CHAKRAS

The Seven Wonders Within

The art of becoming pearl divers,
Discovering the pearls within ourselves.

AUTHOR: SHEETAL JHAVERI

CO-AUTHOR: AASHI KHATRI

CONTENTS

FOREWORD I

Imagine you had a tool that could transform your life drastically—not just your physical health, but also your wealth, relationships, and career. What if I told you that you could overcome all your hurdles to happiness? What if you could live in a world where joy is not just a guest but a permanent resident in your heart?

We often feel that something is missing in our lives. But what is it, really? The truth is, we're not living up to our full potential. Take my word—if one doesn't live up to their potential (and not everyone does!), they should work towards it, because in the end, that's what really matters. This is the core lesson of this book. The key is to become the best version of ourselves, the version we are destined to be!

Deep inside us, there are powerful secrets that can help us rise above difficulties, find peace and acceptance, even when things are tough.

This book is for everyone striving for growth, for those in search of inner peace. It's for those who have everything yet feel that something is missing; it's for those who want to help others and themselves. It's for those who sense the existence of a power within and around them, but don't know what it is. This book has answers for everyone who is ready to rise higher than where they are.

The authors' view on life is simple: balance your chakras and let the rest unfold naturally! Sheetal Jhaveri is the wise Sudha who guides and inspires Aashi, always curious like Aarohi. The work in the coming pages isn't just a snippet of information—it's something that will stay with you for the rest of your life, bringing massive and lasting change. It can make your life easier and more effortless.

If you open your eyes and look above, you'll see the sky, but if you close your eyes and look within, you will see the whole universe.

This book is a work of art! The whole scenic experience is real; everything happens right in front of your eyes! This way of presenting spiritual science is unique. One gets entrapped in awe and realisation, even while reading. This is one of those books you'll want to revisit again and again. So, get ready to create a huge impact on your life. Make sure to take a deep breath, and with a smile, we begin!

– Dr. Maya H. Thakor

Ayurvedic Practitioner,

Surat, Gujarat.

FOREWORD II

In today's fast-paced, automated era, the importance of mental health cannot be overstated. Amidst the relentless demands and distractions, we often lose touch with the core of our being. This book presents a fragrant bouquet of peace, calmness, and self-awareness, drawing on rich cultural traditions that provide a timeless path to inner peace.

Meditation, as this book beautifully illustrates, is the key to handling life's challenges with grace and composure. It is a practice that not only promotes tranquillity but also encourages a solution-oriented approach to problems. Meditation takes us on a journey of self-discovery, helping us uncover our true purpose and attain a sense of completeness and clarity.

The teachings in this book guide you towards achieving your goals by aligning your body and mind. It offers insights on how to heal from within, promoting harmony and balance that are essential for overall wellbeing. This holistic approach ensures that every aspect of your life, from personal aspirations to professional endeavours, benefits from a calm and focused mind.

For anyone seeking to enhance their mental and emotional health, this book is an invaluable resource. It helps you understand how to nurture your inner self, fostering resilience and strength. The wisdom contained within these pages is not only beneficial but essential for all human beings striving to navigate the complexities of modern life.

Welcome to a journey of profound transformation, where peace, clarity, and self-awareness become your guiding principles. This book is your companion on the path to a harmonious and fulfilling life, offering timeless wisdom that resonates across cultures and traditions. Embrace this opportunity to connect with your inner self and discover the boundless potential that lies within.

– Rimple R. Popat

Assistant Professor,

Ahmedabad, Gujarat.

Chapter 1

PURSUIT OF WISDOM

Aarohi had always felt a strange pull, an indescribable force that echoed within her like a silent song. It was a curiosity about things that others seemed to overlook, an eagerness to learn about the mysterious, the mystic, and the unseen. The answers to her questions often came up short, even in the vast maze of the internet. She longed to comprehend the hidden threads that wove the fabric of life, an understanding she suspected was beyond the reach of conventional knowledge.

One humid summer afternoon, she found herself in a dusty antique bookstore in a forgotten corner of town. The walls had dark wooden shelves. They seemed tired from holding centuries-old knowledge. There, among discarded volumes of old books, a tattered book about 'Chakras' caught her attention. Aarohi's heart throbbed in anticipation as she flipped through its timeworn pages. It was full of strange symbols, diagrams of lotus-like flowers, and tales of hidden energies.

Intrigued, Aarohi purchased the book and started a quest that would lead her towards a deeper understanding of herself and the world around her. However, the book, while engaging, was challenging to comprehend. Theories, while fascinating, were abstract. Practices seemed impossible to attempt alone. She felt lost, like a ship lost in the middle of the sea.

Aarohi Oberoi, a bright and ambitious 23-year-old, is a software engineer by profession. Born and raised in the serene city of Weyburn, Saskatchewan, Canada, she was a living embodiment of determination and intellectual curiosity. Aarohi had a natural flair for solving complex problems and devising innovative solutions in the ever-evolving world of technology.

From a young age, Aarohi was deeply career-oriented, driven by a passion to excel in her field. Her days were often spent immersed in lines of code, finding joy in the creation and innovation that her work allowed. She thrived in the logical and structured world of software engineering, where every problem had a solution waiting to be discovered.

Despite her deep involvement in the world of technology, Aarohi harboured an intriguing fascination for something seemingly at odds with her professional life: her deep-seated curiosity about the mysteries of the universe. Intrigued by the notion of a hidden supernatural force, she longed to uncover its secrets. This fascination was a stark contrast to her daily life as a software engineer, where logic and reason reigned supreme. Yet, it was this very contrast that made her journey so unique.

This quest for understanding led her to Rishikesh, India, a place known as the spiritual heartland. She felt as if she would get all her answers there. Determined, she requested a fortnight's leave from her job and embarked on her journey. She boarded a flight to Delhi and then took a bus to Rishikesh. Nestled in the foothills of the Himalayas along the banks of the River Ganga, Rishikesh is renowned for its spiritual significance.

Upon her arrival in Rishikesh, she found the surroundings to be overly crowded. Disappointed, she thought that she had come to a wrong place. Anyway, she settled into a hotel, had a quiet dinner, and rested. The following morning, Aarohi woke up with the sun and took an autorickshaw to the sacred banks of the river Ganga.

Aarohi sat on the smooth, river-washed stones of the Ganga's bank. Children were laughing and splashing each other, while vendors were setting up their stalls for the day.

Aarohi was a silent observer amidst the symphony of life unfolding around her, lost in the depth of her thoughts. As she gazed into eternity, the book lay unopened in her lap. She heard a faraway voice which said, "What if I tell you, there is a magical factory in our city?" The word 'magical' caught her attention, and she immediately turned behind to look where it was coming from.

She saw a lady surrounded by a group of students. Aarohi stood up and started moving towards her. As she moved closer, she saw the lady's eyes shimmering with wisdom and warmth. A captivating smile graced her lips, showcasing her genuine happiness and inner tranquillity. This exceptional glow on her face, however, was beyond mere physical attributes. It was her inner beauty that shone through, reflecting her life's experiences and a deep sense of self-acceptance. This radiance also came from a well-nurtured spirit, rooted in self-love, compassion, and an unwavering belief in her own worth.

The lady, Sudha, noticed the curiosity in Aarohi's eyes and gestured to her to join the students. "Let me tell you a secret!" Sudha said, her voice painting pictures in the cool refreshing air, "that there exists a magical factory here in our city. This is no ordinary factory; its terrace possesses a power so compelling and miraculous that whatever you ask for there, under the open sky, comes true."

A hushed silence fell over the gathered students as they absorbed this exciting concept.

"But every magical tale has its challenges," Sudha continued, with a twinkle in her eye. "This factory is guarded by a watchman, Hari, a gatekeeper of dreams. He doesn't let just anyone enter those mystical doors. You can't step inside unless Hari permits you. You must persuade him."

She paused, letting the words sink in. The idea of a wish-fulfilling terrace tempted them, but Hari, the watchman, was an unexpected obstacle.

"Yet, wouldn't you want to see this charm for yourself?" Sudha asked. "Wouldn't the lure of the magic compel you to convince the watchman? To gain access to a place where your every wish, your every desire could become reality?"

A collective "Yes" rippled through the students, each of them already envisioning their wishes coming true.

Sudha nodded, "Good. Now, how does one convince Hari? Well, he has his preferences. He allows those who are persistent, those who visit repeatedly and regularly.

He respects those who can clearly visualise their wishes, who bring a distinct image or a vivid video of what they truly want. And most importantly, he appreciates those who attach heartfelt emotions to their desires, especially happiness."

"Our emotions emit specific vibrational frequencies," Sudha continued as she unfolded a chart and displayed it to the students. "The magical terrace provides us with things that match the frequency at which we vibrate; the higher the frequency, the better things we receive. Here's a vibrational frequency chart of emotions by David R. Hawkins for your reference. Let's aim at vibrating at the frequency of 'Joy' for now—imagine what makes you happy, and feel this emotion deeply."

Name of level	Energetic log
Enlightenment	700-1000
Peace	600
Joy	540
Love	500
Reason	400
Acceptance	350
Willingness	310
Neutrality	250
Courage	200
Pride	175
Anger	150
Desire	125

(Contd.,)

Name of level	Energetic log
Fear	100
Grief	75
Apathy	50
Guilt	30
Shame	20

Table 1: Energetic Log of Emotions

Sudha asked, "So, are you all ready to convince Hari?"

"Yes!" The response from her students was unanimous and passionate. The thought of being granted their wishes sent a wave of excitement through them.

Sudha smiled, pleased. "Very well then. Let's set about crafting our plan to convince Hari. I want you to visualise a clear, concise picture of what you deeply desire. Close your eyes, and for the next ten minutes, focus on that image."

Ten minutes later, a student raised a hand, "Ma'am, I'm struggling. I can't seem to visualise it clearly enough to convince Hari."

Sudha nodded, understanding. "That's alright, remember, we live in a world where resources are plentiful. We have full access to the internet. Look up images, videos, whatever helps you create that clear image. Let's keep at it until we've got our keys to convince Hari."

The group of students, guided by Sudha, started crafting their plans to persuade the mythical watchman; their hearts filled with hope, excitement, and the promise of wishes coming true.

After a while, one of the students confidently raised his hand, voicing a curiosity that had been bubbling within. "Ma'am," he began, "I've formed a precise image of my heart's desire in my mind. Now, may I know the exact location of this mystical factory?"

A knowing smile graced Sudha's lips as she replied, "This factory, this magical wish -granting factory, is nothing more than your own subconscious mind."

An air of awe spread as she continued. "Our subconscious mind has a great power, the power to change thoughts into reality. It is capable of taking whatever we imagine, and if we supplement that image with faith, belief, and the emotions, it can change it into reality."

Amazement played on the faces of the students, their eyes wide with the realisation of the power they'd been carrying within them all along. One student, unable to contain his excitement, exclaimed, "When I used to watch superhero movies as a child, I'd always wish I had some superpowers. Today, I feel as if I've always had this superpower, but I just never knew about it. I'm overjoyed. Thank you, ma'am, for unveiling this magical power to us."

Sudha nodded, a soft chuckle escaping her. "Precisely. Each one of us harbours this superpower within us, but most people remain unaware of its existence, let alone how to use it to its potential. Now, your task is to tap into the powers of your subconscious mind. We'll discuss your progress in our next class."

A collective "Okay, Ma'am" echoed, and the students began to disperse, their minds abuzz with newfound knowledge and anticipation. However, Aarohi lingered behind. There was a sense of peace, a comforting presence in Sudha that made Aarohi feel as if she had found someone who could finally quench her thirst for knowledge. It was as if she had taken the first step in a long journey, one that promised to uncover truths she'd been seeking all her life. The mysteries of the mind, the enchanting dance of the chakras, and the dormant powers within herself now beckoned her, and she was ready to answer their call.

Sensing Aarohi's confusion and thirst for understanding, Sudha silently took a seat next to her.

"I see you're trying to uncover the secrets of the Chakras," she said, pointing at the book on Aarohi's lap. "It's not a journey one should undertake alone."

Aarohi looked at the lady, a mixture of surprise and relief washing over her. Aarohi confessed her struggles, her search, and her yearning to understand the mysteries of the chakras. Sudha, ever patient, listened attentively, her gaze brimming with empathy.

"The wisdom you seek is not easily found, young girl," she said gently. "The path to understanding the chakras is a deeply personal one, a journey inward towards the very essence of your being. It is a dance between matter and spirit, between the visible and invisible, and between the known and the unknown."

Aarohi felt a rush of excitement. Sudha, sensing the young girl's eagerness, extended an offer. "I can help you navigate this mystical journey, but you must be willing to venture beyond the realm of the known and into the landscape of your own spirit."

With a renewed sense of purpose, Aarohi agreed, and thus began their journey together—a partnership that would take her beyond the threshold of knowledge, deep into the universe within herself, guided by the wisdom of her teacher and the subtle vibrations of the chakras.

Sudha asked Aarohi to meet her at the same place the next morning, and they would start their journey to unravel the powers of the seven major chakras in the body.

Chapter 2

THE JOURNEY BEGINS

As dawn was breaking over Rishikesh, Aarohi found herself on the banks of the Ganga, sitting before her newly found teacher, Sudha. The sacred river flowed past them, mirroring the purples and oranges of the early morning sky. The serenity of the moment seemed to stand still, and the only sounds breaking the silence were the rhythmic splashing of the water against the shore and the occasional rings of temple bells.

Sudha turned to Aarohi, her eyes glinting in the burgeoning light. "Before we embark on this journey together," she began, her voice as soft as the river breeze, "I must ask you a question. Every seeker embarks on a spiritual journey with a reason, a goal, an intention in mind. What, Aarohi, is your purpose?"

Aarohi, her gaze lost in the serene flow of the Ganga, took a moment to gather her thoughts. She then met Sudha's gaze and said, "I am in search of inner peace. I believe that a spiritual awakening can guide me towards it."

Sudha nodded, her face reflecting a gentle understanding. "Indeed," she replied. "Different individuals are drawn to spirituality for different reasons. Some search for fresh ideas, some aim to better control their emotions, while others hope to escape the clutches of depression. Such things as peace, creativity, and emotional equilibrium can be found in various corners of life - in the melodies of music, in the sanctity of worship, or in the silent solitude. These, however, are temporary. For eternal peace, one must explore the depths of spirituality."

The student tilted her head thoughtfully, then asked, "But what about our other aims and goals that are career-oriented or personal? Does spirituality have any connection with these too?"

Her teacher responded with a smile, "Ah, a good question. You see, when we set out with a strong aim, be it career-related or about building strong relationships, the universe assists us. But it doesn't hand things over easily; it shows us the path where we should put efforts. But walking on that path is our job. Not everyone's desires are fulfilled. Have you ever wondered why?"

Aarohi shrugged, "Most people don't work hard enough."

"Yes, hard work is crucial," Sudha agreed. "But have you seen construction workers? They work hard all day long only to end up doing the same thing for their entire life. Hard work must be complemented by smart work, discipline, faith in oneself, and many other things. Let's go into more detail.

Firstly, when you want to achieve something, it's important to set a specific timeline. If your goal is to save up one crore rupees, you should decide how long you'll give yourself to reach that goal, maybe three or five years." Aarohi replied, "Setting a timeline seems like a practical way to give ourselves a target and to track progress."

Sudha nodded and continued, "Next, you need to put in the physical effort to make your dreams come true. Being physically and mentally fit plays a big role in success. There's a saying in Hindi, *'Jaisa tan, vaisa man,'* which means that our body and mind are connected. If your body is healthy, your mind is likely to be healthy too, and vice versa. The type of energy you feel inside can depend on your thoughts. If you think negatively, you'll feel negative, but if you think positively, you'll feel positive." Aarohi nodded in agreement and noted it down.

"Your mind has a big role in your life. It takes in everything it hears and sees. It can be hard to control our minds, but it's not impossible. A lot of the time, we focus on the negatives in our experiences, even when there are lots of positives. For example, when thinking about a great trip, you might focus on a relative who was unhappy the whole time. You start with a positive thought, but your mind goes to the one negative thing.

Keep in mind that our minds control our brains. Our subconscious mind doesn't understand 'no' or 'not.' If I tell you not to think of a white elephant, you'll definitely think of a white elephant. When we say, 'I shouldn't get ill,' the sentence is negative even though the intention is positive. So, instead, say, 'I am healthy,' to keep both the sentence and the intention positive."

Aarohi was surprised. "That's a great way to control our mind, especially the negative thoughts."

"Yeah! It's not that we intentionally get negative thoughts," Sudha continued. "But our minds habitually wander aimlessly. We should strive to consciously stop this aimless wandering. Pay attention to your thoughts and observe if they are positive or negative. Take note of your body's posture at the same time."

To demonstrate her point, Sudha proposed a simple experiment. "Sit up straight and close your eyes," she instructed. Aarohi followed her guidance. "Now, remember a time when you felt very sad," Sudha continued. As Aarohi did this, her smile faded, her expression became one of helplessness, and her shoulders slouched.

Sudha then advised Aarohi to open her eyes, take a deep breath, sit up straight again, close her eyes, and recall a moment of great happiness. This time, Aarohi's lips curved into a smile, and her shoulders broadened.

Sudha then explained, "When we're sad or upset, our posture tends to collapse, our shoulders slouch, and our heart rate might increase. But when we're joyful, our posture naturally improves. A person with depression wouldn't typically describe their condition with a beaming smile or an upright posture."

"Since our thoughts can affect our body so much, I wonder if the reverse is also true—can our body influence our thoughts?" Aarohi questioned.

Sudha emphasised the deep connection between mind and body. "Each affects the other. Controlling the mind is complex, but we can start with regulating our body. By consciously maintaining an upright posture and a smile, we can navigate our thoughts away from negativity."

To further illustrate her point, she suggested another experiment: "Try to recall a sad memory while keeping a genuine smile on your face."

Aarohi responded, "Ah, I am only able to manage one at a time, not both."

"Exactly," Sudha affirmed. "It's challenging to do both because our mind and body are so intricately connected that they are unable to move in opposite directions at one time. This demonstrates that by adjusting our physical state, we can guide our mind's agility and change our thoughts," she explained.

Aarohi, having learned about the intricate dance between her thoughts and physical state, nodded appreciatively.

"Where are the other students today?" Aarohi asked softly. "They have planned a trip to Kedarnath for a few days, so they will be departing today," Sudha explained. "Wow, that's amazing," Aarohi responded, her eyes lighting up with excitement. Sudha's smile broadened, warmed by Aarohi's enthusiastic reaction.

As the sun climbed higher in the sky, casting its warm glow over the Ganges, the lesson lingered in Aarohi's mind. Sudha had to leave, but Aarohi sat there on the riverbank, her eyes tracing the gentle flow of the water, pondering the deep insights Sudha had shared. The interplay of mind and body, the importance of positive thinking, and the significance of smart work alongside hard work – these concepts swirled in her thoughts like the whirlpool in the river.

Aarohi realised that her journey towards inner peace and success was not just a spiritual quest but also a practical one.

It involved setting clear goals, timelines, and understanding the subtle but powerful connection between her physical state and her thoughts. As she reflected, she felt a strong determination to incorporate these lessons into her life.

She visualised her future, imagining herself achieving her goals, both personal and professional. She envisioned herself practising the discipline and mindfulness Sudha had spoken of, ensuring her thoughts and actions were aligned with her aspirations. The realisation that her journey was both an inward and outward one filled her with a sense of purpose.

As the day began to ascend, Aarohi stood up, feeling a sense of clarity and direction. She looked forward to meeting Sudha the next day, eager to delve deeper into the wisdom her teacher had to offer.

Walking away from the riverbank, Aarohi carried with her not just the teachings of her mentor but also a sense of responsibility towards herself and her journey. She understood that the path to enlightenment and success was a continuous one, requiring consistent effort, introspection, and a harmonious balance between the mind and the body.

With these thoughts and the peaceful sounds of the Ganges echoing in her heart, Aarohi made her way to the hotel, ready to set out on a new day and a new chapter in her life, guided by the wisdom she had received and the lessons she was yet to learn.

Chapter 3

KUNDALINI SHAKTI

The following day, the duo met again. Aarohi, brimming with excitement, was eagerly waiting for what Sudha had to teach that day. They found a quiet place near the shores of the Ganges, away from the hustle and bustle of the crowds.

Aarohi eagerly began, "Ma'am, I've spent the entire night wondering what knowledge I'll gain from you today. I'm curious about the path this journey will unfold." Sudha smiled, her eyes reflecting the calmness of the morning. In tune with Aarohi's enthusiasm, Sudha advised, "Don't chase the outcome; relish every step of the journey." She then began with the day's lesson.

"According to Hindu mythology," Sudha explained, "Brahma, the creator of the world, brought forth the earth, the sky, insects, animals, and finally, humans. To these humans, he granted a unique power, a boon known in Hindi as 'Vardaan', a gift so potent that it could not be revoked. Yet, with this power, humans began to cause destruction, slowly damaging everything they touched. Brahma got upset with the reckless use of this gift, so he decided to hide the power away.

He considered hiding it in various locations, such as the towering heights of the Himalayas, but it became apparent that humans would find it anyhow, from anywhere. Eventually, Brahma realised the perfect hiding place was within the humans themselves. They would search far and wide, searching every inch of the earth, but rarely would they consider looking inward. Thus, he concealed this mighty power inside them, where it came to be known as Kundalini."

Aarohi's eyes widened in astonishment. She had been raised on a diet of mythological tales, but none had hinted at such an immense power residing within her. With a mix of awe and disbelief, she stuttered, "Are you implying, all this time, we have had this...this remarkable power concealed within us?"

"Yes, Aarohi," her teacher responded, her eyes glinting with a knowing look. "We hold within us an immense, latent energy, capable of transforming our lives. Kundalini Shakti, also referred to as the Serpentine Power, isn't a literal snake coiled within us. It is a power which is imagined to be awakened in the shape of a snake. To awaken the Kundalini Shakti, our chakras must be in balance. Until then, this power remains dormant within us."

"The Kundalini Shakti first awakens the individual, then itself," Sudha continued. "As one begins their spiritual journey, they may encounter a spectrum of new and unusual experiences. These changes can be felt physically, mentally, or emotionally."

This revelation shook Aarohi's world, causing her to reevaluate the potential of her own existence. It was as if she was staring at an abstract painting she had seen countless times before, but was now beginning to understand the hidden depth behind the seemingly simple lines and strokes.

As this enlightening session drew to a close, her teacher left her with a thought to ponder. "Remember, Aarohi," she cautioned, "the journey of balancing chakras is a journey of self-discovery, acceptance, and transformation. It is a path that demands dedication, discipline, and patience. But those who tread this path can achieve inner peace and personal growth beyond their wildest dreams."

Aarohi was eager to awaken the dormant power that resided in her, to explore the mysteries of Kundalini. She looked at her teacher, her heart pounding with excitement and apprehension. "I am ready, Ma'am. I am ready."

Chapter 4

INTRODUCTION TO CHAKRAS

At the break of dawn, near the serene Ganges, Aarohi met Sudha at their usual spot. The air was filled with a sense of tranquillity, perfect for the day's lesson. Aarohi, with her notebook ready and her mind open, looked at Sudha with eager anticipation. "Good morning, Ma'am," she greeted warmly.

"Good morning, Aarohi," Sudha responded, her voice steady and soothing. "Today is a significant day in your journey. We will start exploring the very essence of what chakras are and their remarkable impact on our lives."

Aarohi smiled, her eyes lighting up with curiosity. "I'm so excited to learn about chakras," she said, her voice brimming with eagerness. "Understanding their true significance feels like beginning an important chapter in my spiritual quest."

"Yes, you are right. To understand what chakras are, it's important to know about nadis first," Sudha began. "In the vast, complex network of our body, there exist over 72,000 'nadis' or channels through which life force energy (prana) passes. These nadis intersect at various points, creating a triangle-shaped convergence. These pivotal junctions are referred to as 'chakras'."

Aarohi jotted down notes, her curiosity growing. "And these chakras, they're triangles, not circles as the name suggests?"

"Exactly," Sudha nodded. "Though 'chakra' means 'wheel', they are actually triangular energy channels. Out of the 114 chakras that exist in our body, seven are recognised as the most significant - they correspond to the seven major endocrine glands."

Sudha paused, ensuring Aarohi was keeping up. "Among the numerous *nadis*, the three most significant are *Ida*, *Pingala*, and *Sushumna*. *Ida* lies to the left of the spine, whereas *Pingala* is to the right side of the spine and *Sushumna* runs along the spinal cord in the centre."

"Can you explain more about these three *nadis*?" Aarohi asked.

"Of course," Sudha replied, eager to share her knowledge. "*Ida* and *Pingala* symbolise life's duality. *Ida* is often associated with feminine and lunar qualities, earning it the name *Chandra Nadi*. In contrast, *Pingala* represents masculine and solar attributes, known also as *Surya Nadi*. Interestingly, our breath plays a key role in the energy flow through these *nadis*. When we breathe predominantly through our left nostril, it indicates the activation of *Chandra Nadi*, reflecting a state of calmness and tranquillity. On the other hand, breathing through the right nostril signifies the activation of *Surya Nadi*."

Curious, Aarohi paused to notice her own breathing. "It seems I'm currently breathing through my left nostril," she observed.

Sudha nodded with a smile. "That means your *Chandra Nadi* is active, representing a calm and peaceful state. These *nadis* alternate approximately every 90 minutes, creating a balance within our bodies. Talking about the third important *nadi*, *Sushumna*, is like a blank canvas. It is full of potential, as it has no quality of its own. When energy flows through *Ida* and *Pingala*, we're influenced by external factors. But when it flows through *Sushumna*, we achieve inner stability and balance and we do not get affected much by the external world. When theseven major chakras are unblocked, the energy of Kundalini uncoils and rises up the *Sushumna* from the base of the spine and moves to *Sahasrara*, the top of the head."

Aarohi's eyes lit up with understanding. "So, does our breath play a vital role in balancing these seven major chakras?"

"Indeed," Sudha replied. "Our breath, the life-giving rhythm of inhalation and exhalation, ensures the effective pumping of blood which, in turn, generates energy. This energy needs to flow freely through our body to facilitate the proper functioning of glands and balancing the chakras."

"Sometimes, it's this very energy that brings about miraculous recoveries in extremely difficult medical situations," Sudha continued. "Doctors might lose hope, but a patient's willpower, fuelled by this energy, can overcome the odds. Willpower, a product of the mind, is at its peak when the energy flow is harmonious."

"I see," Aarohi pondered. "So, balancing these chakras can unlock our hidden potential?"

"Yes," Sudha responded. "But this is only possible when both mind and body are in a state of balance. If either is disturbed, the focus is lost, and the fullest enjoyment of life remains unattained.

The ability to manifest our desires into reality demands discovering these hidden talents. This discovery is achievable when the mind is under our command, made possible by controlling our body physiology. When the mind is under our control, we start seeing the universe in a new light and are blessed with brilliant ideas."

Aarohi absorbed Sudha's words, the early morning light reflecting her growing enlightenment. As the river flowed gently beside them, it seemed to mirror the flow of energy they discussed, an endless stream of potential and discovery.

"The seven major chakras about which we are going to learn in the upcoming sessions are: Muladhara Chakra, Swadhistana Chakra, Manipura Chakra, Anahata Chakra, Vishuddhi Chakra, Agya Chakra and Sahasrara Chakra. Starting from the base of the spine till the top of the head, each chakra is associated with different aspects of our physical, emotional, and spiritual wellbeing. Balancing these chakras is key to harmonising our physical, emotional, and spiritual selves."

"And to be the best version of ourselves," Aarohi added. Sudha smiled and nodded in appreciation.

As the morning's lesson drew to a close, Aarohi's notebook was filled with insightful notes. Sudha, observing

Aarohi's deep contemplation, knew that the seeds of wisdom she planted today had found fertile ground. Already anticipating the next lesson, Aarohi said, "I can't wait to continue our discussions, Ma'am. The knowledge you share is invaluable to me."

Sudha smiled warmly. "Let us meet again tomorrow at dawn. The early morning, with its beautiful environment, is the perfect backdrop for our lessons. It helps us connect more deeply with ourselves and the universe around us."

Aarohi agreed wholeheartedly. "I'll be here, Sudha Ma'am. This place, at this time, it's like heaven for me."

As they stood up, the serene ambience of the Ganges seemed to bless their commitment to growth and learning. Aarohi's heart was full of gratitude for Sudha, her mentor and guide in this spiritual journey.

With a final look at the serene river, they parted ways, each absorbed in their thoughts, yet connected by the enlightening journey they were undertaking together. The Ganges continued to flow gently, a timeless witness to their spiritual quest, as Aarohi and Sudha looked forward to another enlightening day at the break of dawn.

Chapter 5

ACHIEVING INNER SYMPHONY: WHY ALIGN CHAKRAS

As the first light of the day cast a serene glow over Rishikesh, Aarohi sat in contemplative silence beside Sudha, her mentor. The majestic landscape of the early morning provided a harmonious setting for their spiritual discourse. Aarohi was beginning to grasp the significance of the energy centres within her body. But a thought was buzzing at the back of her mind. Curiosity bubbled within her, and she couldn't resist asking Sudha, "I'm starting to understand that these chakras, when aligned, play a crucial role in the Kundalini awakening. But, is there more to chakra balancing than just that? Is there a broader impact on our life and wellbeing?"

Sudha, understanding the depth of Aarohi's question, gently smiled as she looked at her eager student. Her eyes shone with wisdom as she began to speak, "Yes, Aarohi. There's indeed much more. Chakra balancing isn't just about the Kundalini awakening. It affects many aspects of our life, touching each corner with its profound influence. Let's delve deeper into this."

- Emotional Healing:

  Balanced chakras can provide emotional stability, aiding in healing from past traumas or hurts. They help us to process and release negative emotions, leading to emotional resilience.

- Achieving Goals:

  Balanced chakras create a clear channel for energy flow, aiding in manifesting our desires and reaching our goals. They help align our thoughts, actions, and beliefs with our objectives, thereby enhancing our ability to achieve them.

- Improving Relationships:

  Balancing chakras helps us to understand others and their perspective, to accept them as they are, to be empathetic, leading to healthier and more fulfilling relationships.

- Problem-Solving and Analysis:

  By balancing our chakras, we enhance our ability to understand the root causes of problems. This improved insight allows us to approach solutions more creatively and effectively. By optimising the flow of energy and enhancing our perspective, balanced chakras improve our ability to handle day-to-day problems. They offer clarity, enable us to approach issues from various angles, and facilitate effective resolution.

- Understanding Self:

  By balancing our chakras, we gain a deeper understanding of ourselves, our motivations, and our purpose. It promotes self-awareness and introspection. It gives us an insight into our behavioural patterns, encourages us to observe our thoughts, emotions, and actions non-judgmentally, which can lead to insightful self-discovery and growth.

- Decision-Making:

With the chakras in balance, we can improve our decision-making ability. It provides clarity of thought and perception, helping us make informed decisions that align with our life's goals.

- Developing Forgiveness:

When we start a journey within, we understand that everything happens for a reason. So, we find it easier to let go of grudges and forgive, which frees us from negative energy and fosters inner peace.

- Boosting Confidence:

When our energy system is balanced, it boosts our self-esteem and confidence. We become more assertive in our interactions and are more inclined to take positive risks.

- Improving Health:

Our physical, mental, and emotional health affect one another. Knowing about chakras helps us to find the cause of illness and seek a remedy accordingly. Balanced chakras foster overall health and vitality and help us combat stress and illnesses more effectively.

- Enhancing Intuition:

  Balanced chakras amplify our intuition, alerting us to potential harm, guiding us to hear the unsaid, to see the invisible, to experience the unexplained, and a lot more.

- Last but not the least, Kundalini Shakti, the coiled, sleeping serpent power, awakens when the chakras are aligned. It rises from the base chakra; thus, a clean and energised Root Chakra is crucial for its awakening. Kundalini Shakti moves upwards when the chakras are balanced. When the Crown Chakra, the highest chakra, is open, our entire mind and body are in harmony. This balance gives us a sense of fulfilment and joy, a state of contentment regardless of our external circumstances. We feel a sense of divine blessing that transcends material gain or loss.

As Sudha finished, Aarohi said, her mind full of the new insights Sudha had shared, "I understand now, balancing chakras isn't just about spiritual growth; it affects every aspect of our life, doesn't it?"

Sudha nodded in agreement. "Exactly, Aarohi. When we balance our chakras, we balance our life. It's a journey within, to discover our true selves and to live our best lives."

Sudha's words struck a chord within Aarohi, igniting a spark of determination. With this newfound understanding, she was ready to dive deeper into her spiritual quest.

Looking at Aarohi's maturity and ability to comprehend chakras, Sudha felt it was time to acquaint her with specific characteristics and impacts of each chakra. Sudha began, "Now, Aarohi, that we've broadly outlined the importance of balancing chakras, let's begin our journey through the energy centres. We'll start from the base, the Root Chakra, and ascend up to the Crown Chakra, understanding each one in detail. Let's meet tomorrow at the same place at 5 a.m."

Aarohi nodded in understanding. She felt a magnetic pull towards this age-old wisdom that had been kept alive by spiritual seekers like Sudha. "Thank you, Ma'am, for agreeing to guide me on this path. I appreciate your patience and wisdom. I will meet you here tomorrow at dawn."

With the tranquil sound of the Ganga flowing beside them and the promise of a new dawn of understanding, they parted ways, looking forward to unravelling the inner potent, one chakra at a time.

Chapter 6

MULADHARA CHAKRA (ROOT CHAKRA)

The first chirping birds signalled the arrival of dawn as Aarohi walked her way along the Ganga's banks in the spiritual city. The air was cool and refreshing, carrying the holiness of the sacred river and the vibration of countless whispered mantras. Sudha, the proficient spiritual guide, was already seated on a worn, flat rock by the edge of the glistening water.

Upon seeing Aarohi approach, Sudha's lips curved into a serene smile. "Good morning, Aarohi. Your punctuality is as steadfast as the flow of the Ganga," she praised, her voice carrying the calmness of the early morning river.

Responding with a respectful bow, Aarohi replied, "Thank you, Ma'am. I look forward to today's lesson." She slipped off her sandals, allowing her feet to touch the cool, moistened sands, and settled down beside Sudha.

Sudha smiled and began to unfold the mysteries of the chakras, one by one, guiding Aarohi on the path of deep self-discovery and inner harmony.

She opened a chart that looked as follows:

Glands	Adrenal glands
Element	Earth
Location	On the tailbone of the spine
Colour	Red
Deity	Ganesha, Brahmaji
Animal Totem	Snake
No. of Petals	4
Celestial body *(Graha)*	Mars
Seed Syllable *(Beej Mantra)*	*Lam*
Organs	Bones, legs, feet, lower back.
Sense	Smell
Food	Apple, beetroot

Table 2: Muladhara Chakra

She explained, "For all the chakras, I will show you a similar chart. This chart not only mentions the specific gland linked to each chakra but also highlights the element of nature, colour, deity, and animal totem associated with it. Moreover, it includes the corresponding celestial body, which offers insights into the cosmic influences on the chakra.

Additionally, the chart specifies the sense and organs connected to each chakra, providing a clearer understanding of its physical and sensory aspects. The chart also mentions the location of each chakra within the body, as well as the number of petals it possesses—a symbolic representation of its qualities. It specifies a seed or core *mantra* as well. The recitation of these *mantras* aids in activating the chakras. Finally, the chart lists specific foods that can help balance each chakra."

"Can you please explain how these are related to the chakras in detail?" asked Aarohi.

"Certainly, I'd be happy to delve into the details of the chakra and its interrelation with these aspects," Sudha replied. She began, "Residing at the base of our spine, at the tailbone, the Muladhara Chakra, also known as the Root Chakra, holds the primal energy connecting us to our physical existence. It governs the fundamental necessities of life such as sleep, food, water, physical needs, and financial stability. Like a tree gets nourishment and stability from its roots, our Root Chakra revolves around our physical nourishment and financial stability.

As we know, all matter is composed of five basic elements: Earth, Water, Fire, Air, and Space. These are also known as '*Pancha Mahabhutas*'. The human body is also made up of these elements.

The first five chakras: Muladhara, Swadhisthana, Manipura, Anahata, and Vishuddhi are associated with the physical elements earth, water, fire, air, and ether (or space) respectively. The last two chakras, Agya and Sahasrara, are thought to connect us beyond the earthly realm, so they are associated with the elements of light and thoughts respectively.

Earth, the element of the Root Chakra, signifies our primal connection with it. We stand and walk on the earth with our feet, symbolising our connection with this element. In the end, we return to the earth, completing the cycle of life and death."

"How intricately we are connected to nature!" the young girl exclaimed. "When you mention the term 'chakras', you are referring to the seven major chakras, right?" she confirmed.

"Yes," Sudha affirmed and continued with her explanation. "As previously stated, the seven major chakras each correspond to a specific endocrine gland. The Root Chakra is associated with the adrenal glands.

An imbalance in the Muladhara Chakra disrupts essential needs such as sleep, physical nourishment, and financial stability. Adrenal glands produce hormones that help regulate metabolism, the immune system, blood pressure, response to stress, and other essential functions. Imbalance in the Root Chakra might lead to improper functioning of adrenal glands, leading to a lack of energy and easy fatigue. Consequently, maintaining a robust immunity becomes crucial for the organs associated with this chakra. Calcium plays a pivotal role in strengthening our bones, which form the physical foundation of our being. Foods like apples, beetroot, and pomegranate, abundant in iron, can aid in balancing this chakra."

"It also resonates with the feeling of consuming something healthful and nourishing," Aarohi reflected. Looking at the symbol of the Root Chakra on the chart, she wondered, "What is this strange symbol, and does it hold a deeper meaning?"

Sudha nodded, "The chakras are associated with distinct symbols that hold significant meaning. Many of these symbols feature inverted triangles and intricate lotus petals. These components are not just decorative elements, but they carry deeper symbolism that can help us unravel their significance. Let's learn about the symbol of Muladhara Chakra.

The four petals of the Muladhara Chakra symbolise the four fundamental pillars of our existence:

PETALS OF THE MULADHARA CHAKRA:

- Dharma - To understand the moral values and virtues of our religion.

- Artha - To pursue wealth through righteous and ethical means.

- Karma - The actions we take while following our Dharma.

- Moksha - The 'liberation from rebirth' achieved through our karma.

These four petals represent the four phases of our life: *Brahmacharya Ashram, Grihastha Ashram, Vanaprastha Ashram,* and *Sanyasa Ashram.* These are the four pillars of a balanced life."

Aarohi's eyes widened in fascination as Sudha shared the meaning behind the symbols. "It's incredible," she exclaimed. "It's like a roadmap for understanding our existence. I am wondering how I would know if my Root Chakra is balanced or not?"

Sudha illustrated, "When the Muladhara, or Root Chakra, is blocked, individuals often go through the following:"

INDICATORS OF AN IMBALANCED MULADHARA CHAKRA:

◆ Feeling unsafe and insecure about their life paths.

◆ Financial instability.

◆ Sleeplessness

◆ Regular occurrences of lower back pain.

"To elaborate, financial stability and the efficient management of resources contribute to a sense of security and peace. These factors also influence your dietary habits, which in turn impact your overall health. If these elements are missing, a feeling of unworthiness can arise due to the inability to afford even basic necessities, leading to possible dependence on others."

"I think everyone's definition of 'basic needs' differs. What might be a luxury to one person could be a necessity to another," Aarohi reflected.

"You are right," acknowledged Sudha. "Having the means to satisfy one's basic needs, whatever they may be, indicates a balanced Root Chakra. A Gujarati saying, *"Naana vagar no Nathiyo, naane Nathalal"*, aptly expresses the importance of wealth in society. It implies that a person's respectability often increases with their financial stability and proper management of money."

"Pondering over the points you mentioned, I think my Root Chakra may not be blocked. But to deepen my understanding, could you provide insights on how it feels when this chakra is open?" inquired Aarohi.

"Sure!" Sudha responded. "When the Root Chakra is open, individuals generally exhibit the following:"

INDICATORS OF A BALANCED MULADHARA CHAKRA:

- A healthy level of confidence regarding financial matters.

- Feeling secure and content with your body.

- Maintaining strong relationships with your friends and family. In this state, individuals earn respect from others and cultivate a strong sense of self-worth.

Aarohi listened intently, her eyes reflecting a dawning understanding. "So, it's not just about unblocking the chakra but also nurturing it continuously," she mused aloud. The concept of an open Root Chakra resonated with her newly acquired understanding of balance and wellbeing. She pondered on Sudha's words about financial confidence and physical security, realising how these aspects were intertwined with her sense of stability. "It seems that nurturing the Root Chakra is about fostering a holistic sense of security and grounding in various aspects of life," Aarohi concluded thoughtfully.

"Right," Sudha further explained. "Most chakras have some emotions related to them; these emotions get affected by the state of the chakra. The emotions revolving around the Root Chakra are:"

EMOTIONS ASSOCIATED WITH THE MULADHARA CHAKRA:

- Survival

- Security

- Insecurity

Aarohi's curiosity was now piqued further. She asked, "Are there any specific ways in which we can balance our Root Chakra?"

Sudha explained firmly, "To maintain a healthy Root Chakra, consider practising the following exercises:"

ACTIVITIES TO BALANCE THE MULADHARA CHAKRA:

- Manage your finances.

- Gardening

- Jogging

- Walking barefoot

- Feet tapping

- Bridge pose

◆ Garland pose

◆ Affirmations:

  • I have a healthy body.

  • I am safe, protected, and secure.

  • I am proud of myself.

  • I have everything I need.

◆ Chanting the *'Beej Mantra'*:

  The mantra to activate the Root Chakra is *'Lam'*. When we recite this mantra, its vibrations reach the Root Chakra and activate it.

"One of the most essential things for our survival is oxygen. Adequate oxygen intake is important for the health of the mind and body. It is important that sufficient oxygen reaches the Root Chakra."

Illustration 1: Malasana (Garland Pose)

Aarohi was beginning to understand that chakra balancing was a multifaceted practice, encompassing various elements of daily life.

"In essence," the wise lady summarised, "the Muladhara Chakra is about grounding ourselves in the reality of our physical existence and mastering our basic needs, thereby setting a firm foundation for our spiritual journey. With this comprehensive understanding of the Muladhara, we are now prepared to ascend the ladder of spiritual awakening, moving upwards towards the next chakra, discovering the ways they interlink, and further enhancing our holistic wellbeing."

Chapter 7

SWADHISTHANA CHAKRA (SACRAL CHAKRA)

As the sun ascended in the sky and the city awakened, the streets came alive with a vibrant energy, bustling with activity. Sudha asked her bright student, "What do you do in your leisure time? What makes you happy?"

Playing with the sand by the Ganges, Aarohi replied, "I usually learn new things, and sometimes I paint or play video games."

Sudha chuckled softly. "That's wonderful. Finding joy in life is crucial. The next chakra is closely tied to this concept." She continued as she opened a new chart, "Swadhisthana Chakra, also known as the Sacral Chakra, comes into focus once our fundamental needs are satisfied. As we advance beyond the basic necessities, we yearn for more refinement and luxury in life, often driven by creativity. It's this chakra that empowers us to enjoy life's pleasures and helps foster financial prosperity through our creative endeavours."

Glands	Ovaries and Testes
Element	Water
Location	2 inches below the navel
Colour	Orange
Deity	Krishna, Vishnu
Animal Totem	Jaguar
No. of Petals	6
Celestial body *(Graha)*	Moon, Venus
Seed Syllable *(Beej Mantra)*	*Vam*
Organs	Reproductive organs, gallbladder, kidneys, lower back, lower abdominal muscles.
Sense	Taste

(Contd.,)

Food	Orange, Tangerine, good fats rich in Omega-3 and Omega-6 fatty acids, such as chia seeds, flax seeds, sesame seeds, almonds, cashew nuts, and walnuts.

Table 3: Swadhisthana Chakra

Aarohi pondered, "So, it's like moving beyond just survival to actually enjoying life?"

"Absolutely," Sudha replied. "Now let's understand how these things are interrelated. Our sense of wellbeing is deeply intertwined with the ability to create. Creation brings joy, whether it's birthing a new life or innovating an idea. This is where the Sacral Chakra comes into play.

The Sacral Chakra is associated with the following emotions:

EMOTIONS ASSOCIATED WITH THE SWADHISTHANA CHAKRA:

- Abundance.

- Pleasure.

- Luxury

- Creativity.

- Sexual relations

Luxuries in life can indeed contribute to our happiness, and the Sacral Chakra plays a role in shaping our sense of identity. Luxury often provides us with a distinct identity within society. Moreover, the glands associated with this chakra are linked to our gender identity."

Sudha paused for a moment, ensuring Aarohi was following along. "Now, digging deep into the symbol of this chakra, let's understand what its six petals symbolise:"

PETALS OF THE MULADHARA CHAKRA:

- Attachment (*Moh*): Our emotional attachments often lead to expectations and fears of loss. If we are too attached to materialistic things, our Sacral Chakra needs to be balanced.

- Delusion (*Maya*): The physical world and its materialistic appeal can delude us, making us believe that wealth accumulation is life's sole purpose. However, this pursuit is as elusive as a mirage in the desert, always appearing within reach but perpetually distant.

- Doubt: Pursuing creative ventures often leaves us questioning their success. So doubt can easily creep in. This can be avoided by practising consistently and seeking regular feedback to refine your work.

- Ruthlessness: Sometimes, in our quest to achieve our goals, we may neglect values like compassion and empathy. It's important to understand others' feelings and consider the impact our actions have on them.

- Fear: Fear often holds us back in carrying out new endeavours. A renowned Hindi quote, *'Dar ke aage jeet hai,'* aptly conveys that victory lies beyond fear, emphasising how success awaits those who courageously overcome their fears.

♦ Disdain: Disdain is like looking down on someone or something. It's when you feel that you're better than others, or you think something is not worth your time or attention. To overcome this feeling, it's important to try to see the value in others and be humble and open-minded.

The duo moved towards the river and stepped into the water barefoot. They stood still as the sand grains beneath their feet moved with the rhythm of the waves. "There is such a change in the energy when we step into the water, isn't it?" asked the lively young girl. The prudent woman nodded, "Indeed, water is known to cleanse us, to wash away the negativity that keeps clinging to us every now and then."

"The chart you had shown mentioned that the element of this chakra is water. Could you explain that a bit more?" Aarohi asked.

Sudha's explanation flowed as smoothly as the water around them. "The element associated with the Sacral Chakra is water, a crucial element for detoxification, which is a significant aspect of this chakra. Also, just as water takes the shape of its container, the Sacral Chakra has the power to transform individuals through its influence on creativity, by providing a platform for the execution of skills and creativity. In addition, the organs of the Sacral Chakra include kidneys, responsible for the vital task of detoxification."

Aarohi was bewildered to know how the organs and the element of this chakra are so intricately connected to each other.

"Approximately 60% of our bodies are made up of water. Along with creativity, the Sacral Chakra also governs our emotions," Sudha continued.

"How are these two related?" queried the curious girl.

"It's interesting to know that the moon, especially during full moon and new moon days, can affect how we feel," Sudha replied.

"Really? How?" asked the surprised Aarohi.

Sudha explained, "Tides are the rising and falling of sea levels, caused by the gravitational pull of the moon and the sun on earth's oceans. During a full moon and a new moon, the sun, earth, and moon are aligned, and their gravitational forces combine to create higher high tides and lower low tides, known as spring tides. Much like the ebb and flow of the tides, the waters within us are subtly swayed by the moon's gravitational pull. On full moon days, you might notice feeling a bit heavier emotionally, and the same goes for new moon days. It's like a gentle tug-of-war between our feelings and the moon's gravitational pull. This connection shows us how everything in our world, even the moon in the sky, can have a subtle influence on how we feel inside."

Aarohi was awestruck with this enlightening knowledge, her inquisitiveness heightened. Now she wanted to know it all, all at once. "How would I know if my Sacral Chakra is balanced or not?"

Sudha explained softly, "When the Swadhisthana Chakra is blocked, you might notice these signs:"

INDICATORS OF AN IMBALANCED SWADHISTHANA CHAKRA:

♦ You feel a creativity block.

♦ Reduced enjoyment and pleasure in life.

♦ Decreased libido.

♦ Feelings of abuse and confusion.

♦ Low self-esteem and lack of self-worth.

♦ Addiction to excessive food, alcohol, drugs, or medication, often stemming from depression related to suppressed creativity.

♦ Infertility.

♦ Urinary tract infections.

♦ Gallbladder problems

Sudha added gently, "The initial signs of an imbalance in any chakra typically appear psychologically before impacting the body. It's important to notice these early signs so that we can start working on balancing this chakra. When the Swadhisthana Chakra is balanced, you experience the following:

INDICATORS OF A BALANCED SWADHISTHANA CHAKRA:

♦ Feeling pleasure and satisfaction in sexual intimacy.

♦ Healthy reproductive organs.

♦ Enhanced pathways for creativity.

An open Swadhisthana Chakra provides a platform for the individual to express and explore their creative impulses."

Aarohi contemplated the state of her Sacral Chakra. "I believe my Sacral Chakra is also balanced," she reflected. "But once a chakra is balanced, does that mean it will remain balanced forever?"

Sudha shifted her gaze from the flowing river to her student. "No, my dear," she gently replied. "Achieving balance in a chakra doesn't guarantee that it will always stay balanced. It's all about the flow of energy, which is not always the same. It keeps changing every day, every hour. However, when a chakra maintains balance most of the time, we can say that it is balanced. The more it is balanced, the more likely it is to be balanced in the future as well."

"So, how does one go about balancing the Sacral Chakra when it's blocked?" Aarohi inquired.

Sudha elucidated, "To balance the Sacral Chakra, involve yourself in the following activities:"

ACTIVITIES TO BALANCE THE SWADHISTHANA CHAKRA:

- Swinging

- Creative projects

- Solving puzzles like Sudoku.

- Swimming

- Yoga poses like the pelvic thrust, bridge pose, cobra pose

♦ Self-care activities like massages and warm showers.

♦ Regular meditation with a focus on the Sacral Chakra, using the '*Vam*' mantra, is also a powerful tool for keeping this energy centre in harmony.

♦ The following affirmations also help in balancing the Sacral Chakra:

- I am radiant, beautiful, strong, and enjoy a healthy and passionate life.

- I am in touch with my feelings.

- I am a creative being.

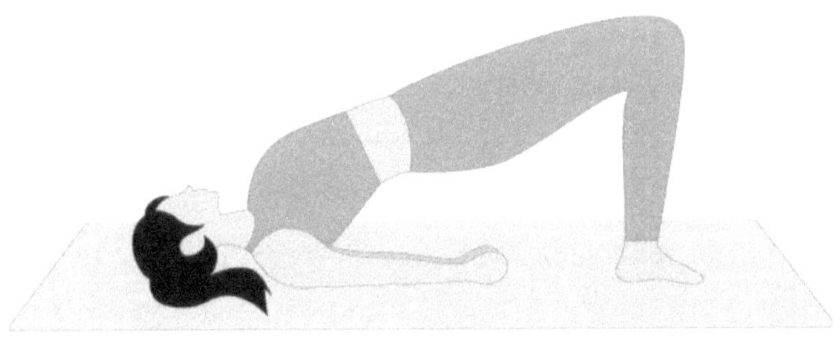

Illustration 2: Setu Bandhasana (Bridge Pose)

As Sudha listed each activity, Aarohi's eyes lit up with recognition. "That's interesting," she said. The suggestion of solving puzzles sparked a hint of surprise and interest in her, a faint smile forming as she imagined herself engaging in all these joyful and self-care activities.

Sudha, pleased with Aarohi's interest, added, "Absolutely, and there's more to it. Along with these activities, consider adding oranges and tangerines to your diet. Doing these activities can greatly assist in rejuvenating your body and spirit, which is essential for nurturing your Sacral Chakra."

Aarohi's eyes widened in surprise. "As we move ahead with balancing each chakra, does the balance or imbalance of the previous chakra have an impact on it?" asked the swift learner.

Sudha nodded, pleased with Aarohi's insightful questions. "All the chakras are interconnected. The more a chakra is balanced, the more strength it provides to balance the subsequent chakras. Let me tell you about the relation of the Sacral and Root Chakras. The Sacral and Root Chakras share a deep connection, particularly in how they influence our creative and foundational energies. The Sacral Chakra is the centre of our creativity, but to effectively harness and express this creativity, a stable foundation is necessary. This foundation is provided by the Root Chakra."

Aarohi reflected, "The Sacral Chakra reminds us that creativity stems from diverse experiences, not monotony. Thus, embracing new experiences is pivotal to stimulating our creative energy and maintaining balance in our Sacral Chakra."

Sudha's eyes twinkled with an adventurous spark. "How about we embrace a new experience right here in Rishikesh? Let's go river rafting!" she suggested enthusiastically.

Aarohi's eyes widened with excitement, a mix of thrill and nervousness flickering in them. "River rafting? Here?" she gasped.

"Yes!" Sudha replied, her voice brimming with energy. "Let's go then," Aarohi said. They both got up to drive to the Tapovan area from where they would register for river rafting. Sudha informed Aarohi that they would go from Brahmpuri to NIM Beach, which was the calmest path of all.

Along the way, Sudha concluded her chapter on Swadhisthana, "The Sacral Chakra is the cradle of creativity, identity, and emotional fulfilment in our lives. It symbolises the transition from fundamental needs to a refined existence, fostering prosperity, pleasure, and a unique sense of self. With its close ties to water, lunar cycles, and creative flow, the Sacral Chakra remains a vibrant force within us. The balance of this chakra leads to a healthy, joyful life, rich in creative expression and sexual satisfaction. As we progress on this spiritual journey, we move towards an understanding of the Solar Plexus Chakra, ascending further on our path to spiritual enlightenment, carrying with us the understanding of the Sacral Chakra's significant role in shaping our identities."

Their instructor was a young, spirited man named Raj. They, along with three more people, were taken to the starting point of Brahmpuri, surrounded by the majestic views of the Himalayas. The Ganges, with its crystal-clear waters, flowed with a gentle ferocity, inviting them into its embrace. The air was crisp and fresh, filling their lungs with a sense of purity and vitality.

Raj equipped them with life jackets and helmets. He briefed them on safety protocols, and as they listened, the rhythmic sound of the river harmonised with the chirping of birds, creating a natural symphony.

As they began their journey, the raft bobbed and swayed with the river's current. Sudha and Aarohi paddled in sync, following Raj's commands. The water splashed around them, cool and refreshing, a stark contrast to the warm sun above.

The rapids were a thrilling dance of nature, each wave a different move. As they navigated through them, Aarohi felt a surge of adrenaline mixed with a deep connection to the water. It was as if the river itself was guiding them, teaching them the art of balance and harmony.

Midway, Raj guided them to a calm spot where they paused. Here, the river was serene, flowing with a gentle grace. Sudha and Aarohi dipped their hands in the water, feeling its soothing touch. They looked around at the lush greenery, the towering mountains, and the clear blue sky. Aarohi observed the stark contrast between her rushed corporate life back in Canada, away from nature. She didn't feel like going back home anymore. She could listen to her heartbeats and felt as if time had stopped. It was a moment of pure bliss, a union of her spirits with nature.

As they approached NIM Beach, the end of their journey, Aarohi felt a sense of accomplishment and renewal. She realised that this experience was not just about thrill and adventure, but about finding harmony within and with the world around her. For the first time, she felt in sync with the world around her. She had always felt that everything around her was moving too fast and trying to catch up; she rushed too, never pausing, never being still.

Sudha smiled at her, a knowing look in her eyes. "See, every new experience adds a layer to our being, enhancing our creativity and our connection with the universe."

As they stepped onto the sandy shores of NIM Beach, they carried with them not just memories of an adventure but lessons from the river – of flow, resilience, and the beauty of embracing life's diverse experiences.

Chapter 8

MANIPURA CHAKRA
(SOLAR PLEXUS CHAKRA)

The next day, the spark of adventure still crackled in the air. Aarohi, wanting to explore more of it, suggested going for a trek. Sudha, her eyes reflecting the same adventurous spirit, agreed spontaneously and said, "Let's pack our bags and set off for Chopta." Aarohi enquired eagerly, "What's Chopta?" Sudha answered, "It is often referred to as 'Mini Switzerland'." Aarohi's eyes lit up in excitement. "Wow! It'll be fun."

As the sun peeked over the surrounding hills, Sudha and Aarohi embarked on a drive towards Chopta. The journey, filled with mesmerising landscapes, was an introduction to the natural splendour that awaited them. Both of them were lost in admiration, captivated by the scenic beauty along the way.

It would be a long drive, so Sudha began with her lesson, "Ascending from the creative waters of the Sacral Chakra, we journey towards the warming fires of the Solar Plexus Chakra or Manipura Chakra. Situated in the stomach area, this chakra symbolises the mental aspect of our existence, representing our ability to understand and process our personal experiences. This transformative chakra is instrumental in refining our wisdom and power, crucial for manifesting our true self and potential. In this lesson, we dive into the intricate workings of the Solar Plexus Chakra, exploring its effects on our decisions, emotions, self-worth, and overall wellbeing."

After a little pause, Sudha continued as she opened a new chart, "The Manipura, or Solar Plexus Chakra, pertains to our perception and understanding of the world. It is symbolic of the 'mind' or *'man'.*"

Gland	Pancreas
Element	Fire
Location	3 inches above the navel
Colour	Yellow
Deity	Ram, Vishnu
Animal Totem	Hummingbird
Petals	10
Celestial body *(Graha)*	Sun
Seed Syllable *(Beej Mantra)*	*Ram*
Organs	Lower back and digestive system: liver, gallbladder, and pancreas.
Sense	Sight
Food	Fibres: corn, whole grains (unpolished), juice (unfiltered)

Table 4: Manipura Chakra

Looking at the chart thoughtfully, Aarohi inquired, "The element associated with this chakra is fire, does it symbolise transformation?"

With a knowing smile, Sudha responded, "Yes, similar to how a seed requires sunlight to grow into a plant, or how water changes state when exposed to heat, the fiery aspect of the Manipura Chakra governs our transformative processes.

Corresponding to the digestive system, this chakra plays a significant role in the digestion of not only food but also in the processing of our experiences and situations. When we struggle to accept certain events or circumstances, or find it difficult to adapt to unexpected or new situations, it indicates a need to balance this chakra."

Aarohi nodded, a hint of nostalgia in her voice. "Oh! That's very relatable. When I was in school, sometimes it was very difficult for me to accept certain things, and I have also seen a lot of people struggling with that. This chakra is very much related to acceptance of reality, right?"

Sudha nodded, "Absolutely, and by practising acceptance, one can more easily move past those struggles."

"True," Aarohi agreed, "I've been doing that, and it has made my life so much easier as I now have more control over my emotions."

Sudha smiled, "Amazing! A balanced Manipura Chakra leads to sound decision-making abilities, fostering self-confidence. Accepting change and maintaining composure during challenging situations are markers of an open Manipura Chakra.

Often when anxious or stressed, we might experience a sensation of our stomach churning. This physical response is linked to the Manipura Chakra."

"Do we feel anxious because we feel powerless in some circumstances?" the observant girl asked.

The wise lady explained, "Yes, Aarohi, power is an important aspect of this chakra. It must be managed wisely. Surrendering our power to others in order to maintain peace isn't always the solution. However, a dominating attitude is equally harmful. We should instead strive to communicate our viewpoint effectively. It's also important sometimes to take things in our control and try to improve them. We should do everything in our power to make our lives better, but when we cannot, we should accept that not everything can be controlled."

Aarohi confirmed, "Understanding what we can control and accepting what we can't are keys to mastering this chakra, is that right?"

Sudha nodded in agreement, feeling proud of how well her student was grasping the lessons. As the landscape outside their window blended into a tapestry of nature's finest, Sudha delved deeper into the essence of the Solar Plexus Chakra, her voice calm and enlightening.

"Imaginary pain," Sudha elaborated, "is an intriguing concept. It's about the distress we cause ourselves by imagining negative outcomes that haven't happened—and might never happen. For instance, worrying that a friend might feel jealous of your success creates a cycle of stress and negativity that's entirely unnecessary."

Aarohi nodded thoughtfully, absorbing the concept. "Similarly, if we imagine how our parents will scold us if we fail in an endeavour, even when the chances of failing are low."

"Exactly," Sudha confirmed. "It's like we're our own worst enemy at times, creating problems in our minds and stressing over events that are unlikely to occur."

Sudha then pointed to the chart detailing the ten petals of the Solar Plexus Chakra. "Each petal represents different aspects that can affect our mental and emotional wellbeing."

PETALS OF THE MANIPURA CHAKRA:

- Spiritual ignorance.

- Thirst

- Jealousy

- Treachery

- Shame

- Fear.

- Disgust.

- Foolishness

- Sadness

- Delusion

"I think most of these feelings arise out of self-doubt," Aarohi remarked thoughtfully. Sudha nodded in agreement, replying, "Yes, you are right. Self-doubt may make us believe that others don't respect us. It's essential to remember that our perspective may not always be accurate. Instead of making assumptions, it's healthier to communicate or reconsider our perspective."

"I agree, I have seen people ending relationships because of their assumptions of what the other person thinks," said Aarohi. "Exactly, but ending a relationship is not always the best thing to do. Instead, addressing the issue with the person can lead to resolution and growth. Unexpressed concerns can lead to lingering guilt, which is counter productive. Balancing the Manipura Chakra is about navigating these complexities with wisdom and grace," explained Sudha.

Sudha continued, "Talking about the emotions associated with it, the Solar Plexus, or Manipura Chakra, revolves around the following emotions:"

EMOTIONS ASSOCIATED WITH THE MANIPURA CHAKRA:

- Self-worth

- Self-respect.

- Self-confidence

- Self-esteem

- Power

- Control

- Decision-making abilities.

- Acceptance of reality

- Expectations

"Its animal totem, the hummingbird, symbolises the wandering and fleeting nature of our mind, isn't it very relatable?" asked Sudha. "Wow! What a metaphor! Our mind has a habit of wandering, but we should not let it control our decisions and actions," Aarohi added aptly.

Sudha, pleased with her student's understanding, said, "Yes, you are right. I must say you are learning very quickly, Aarohi." A warm smile spread across Aarohi's face as she expressed her gratitude to her mentor.

Sudha continued, "Solar Plexus, the transformative chakra, is also affected by digestive fire. The strength of our *Jatharagni'*, or digestive fire, reflects the strength of transformation within us. The stronger the digestive fire, the greater the transformation it results in. On a spiritual level, this fire is recognised as *'Bhutagni'* or the ethereal fire."

She further elaborated, "You know, mythologically, Lord Rama embodies the essence of this chakra through his transformative actions, his establishment of moral order over chaos, and his initiation of monogamy, challenging the polygamy norm. His acceptance and endurance during his 14-year exile demonstrate robust decision-making skills and unwavering resolve, qualities nurtured by a balanced Manipura Chakra."

Reflecting on Sudha's words, Aarohi felt a surge of inspiration. "This is fascinating," she exclaimed, her eyes sparkling with the thrill of discovery. "How does one know if their Manipura is balanced or not?" she asked.

Sudha shared her insights with a gentle voice, "When Manipura Chakra is blocked, you experience the following:

INDICATORS OF AN IMBALANCED MANIPURA CHAKRA:

♦ You feel like a victim in this world.

♦ You feel powerless.

♦ You try to get sympathy.

♦ You either surrender your power to make peace in a relationship or you dominate others.

♦ You suffer from stomach ache and anxiety."

Aarohi absorbed these points and added, "When trapped in difficult situations, self-doubt and victim mentality often arise." Sudha agreed, "Yes, hence we might find ourselves seeking sympathy or surrendering our power, indicative of an imbalanced Manipura Chakra."

Sudha continued, "In contrast, when the Manipura Chakra is open, we experience:"

INDICATORS OF A BALANCED MANIPURA CHAKRA:

♦ A strong sense of authentic power and the knowledge to use it positively.

♦ A great sense of self-worth:

Understanding that we are part of the universal flow, we should strive to give up our ego. Our physical bodies are products of generational influences, and our souls carry experiences from past lives. We cannot separate our existence from this universe. We are connected to the universe in an intricate web, like a network of wires, where every individual is significant. This understanding brings about feelings of worthiness that transcend ego.

For instance, business success is not solely the product of the owner's efforts but also the hard work of employees.

♦ Comfort in setting personal boundaries.

♦ Admiration for those with power and influence, especially those who use their power to positively impact the world:

People often follow societal norms without questioning their origins. However, those with an open Manipura

Chakra admire and accept novelty, while others may react with jealousy or resist new ideas, indicating an imbalance in the Solar Plexus Chakra.

♦ Ability to take action on things that are in our control and acceptance of those beyond our control:

This is a very important aspect of dealing with stress. The first thing to do when you are worried is to check if it is in your control or not. If it is in your control, take action to improve it; otherwise, accept it. Worrying is never a solution. Achieving this balance can lead to substantial personal growth.

Aarohi listened intently, each point Sudha made about the open Manipura Chakra lighting up new pathways in her understanding. The notion of being part of a greater universal flow resonated deeply with her, stirring a sense of connection and purpose. She asked, "How do we balance the Manipura Chakra if it is not?"

Sudha replied, "Let me share some activities to balance the Solar Plexus Chakra:"

ACTIVITIES TO BALANCE THE MANIPURA CHAKRA:

♦ Releasing Anger Constructively:

Anger is a natural emotion, but how we handle it is crucial. Instead of bottling it up or releasing it on anyone, find healthy outlets. For example, writing down your frustrations and then tearing the paper symbolises letting go of those negative emotions. Engaging in physical activities like boxing can also be therapeutic.

You may also count backwards until you calm down, tear old newspapers, or yell out loud, not on others, maybe at an open and empty place. It's important to express anger in a way that doesn't harm others or damage relationships. Think of it as clearing out a vessel filled with negative emotions to make room for positive feelings.

♦ Rock Climbing:

Engaging in rock climbing can be particularly beneficial for the Manipura Chakra. This exercise applies pressure to the stomach area, directly stimulating the Solar Plexus Chakra. It also encourages deep breathing, which is vital for oxygenating the body and promoting clear thinking. During rock climbing, the focus required often leads to a state of mindfulness, allowing you to be more aware of your thoughts, helping you filter the types of thoughts you have.

♦ Altering Daily Routines:

A repetitive routine can lead to a lack of awareness and automatic task execution. By changing up your daily activities, you encourage a state of mindfulness, preventing your mind from falling into autopilot. For instance, when we travel the same route every day, we often reach our destination without much thought. This autopilot mode allows our minds to wander, focusing on other things while walking or driving. Similarly, in fitness, varying your workout routine can maintain mental engagement, as opposed to mindlessly performing the same exercises.

◆ Practising Boat Pose:

   This specific yoga pose is excellent for strengthening the abdominal muscles, which are directly linked to the Solar Plexus Chakra. By engaging these muscles, you're not only promoting physical health but also enhancing the balance of your Manipura Chakra.

◆ Incorporate fibre-rich food into your diet such as corn, unpolished whole grains, and unfiltered juice.

◆ These affirmations also help in balancing the Solar Plexus Chakra:

   • I rule from a place of authentic power and control.

   • I am worthy.

   • I set boundaries with self-care and self-respect.

Aarohi felt a spark of excitement. "It's fascinating to see how interconnected our physical actions and emotional wellbeing truly are."

Sudha replied, "Interconnection reminds me of the interplay between the Sacral and Solar Plexus Chakras. The Sacral Chakra has a significant impact on the Solar Plexus Chakra. When there's a blockage in the Sacral Chakra, it often manifests as a disruption in our creative flow. This disruption can lead to a decrease in self-confidence, which is a key aspect of the Solar Plexus Chakra. Essentially, a balanced Sacral Chakra is crucial for maintaining the confidence and personal power governed by the Solar Plexus Chakra."

"I now understand how important it is to balance Manipura Chakra. It can be particularly empowering in situations where you need confidence, such as voicing your opinion in a family decision. Speaking up, even if your ideas are not adopted, is a vital part of self-expression and maintaining a healthy, balanced chakra. This chakra is the powerhouse of decision-making and emotional maturity. Balancing this chakra allows us to harness our power effectively, fosters self-esteem, and nurtures emotional maturity," reflected Aarohi.

Illustration 3: Navasana (Boat Pose)

"True," Sudha concluded, "The Solar Plexus Chakra, or Manipura, functions as our personal sun, radiating self-worth, power, and transformation from within. It invites us to manage our personal power with wisdom and authenticity, urging us to accept change while understanding the extent of our control over situations. It teaches us to balance concern with unnecessary worry and encourages us to approach life's challenges with grace and confidence. As we continue our journey up the chakra ladder, the next step is the Heart Chakra or Anahata, where we will delve into the realm of love, compassion, and emotional equilibrium. Carrying the warmth and power of the Solar Plexus Chakra, we take our next steps towards enlightenment, embracing the lessons it has bestowed upon us."

The evening in Chopta greeted them with crisp air and lush landscapes. Chopta was a pastoral delight with its meadows and a panoramic view of the Himalayan ranges. It offered a serene backdrop for their spiritual journey.

After soaking in the beauty of the surroundings, they decided to stay closer to nature for the night. They booked a tent amidst greenery, providing them with a connection to the earth beneath and the stars above.

Around them, other trekkers were setting up their tents, each group animated with anticipation for the next day's journey to Tungnath. The air buzzed with the energy of like-minded souls, each drawn to this serene location by the lure of nature and the promise of conquering new heights.

As the night deepened, the campsite became a small community of adventurers sharing stories and experiences around crackling campfires. Aarohi and Sudha joined a group exchanging tales of past treks and the mystical allure of the Himalayas.

As the night wore on, the campsite quieted down, with trekkers retreating into their tents, conserving energy for the early morning start. They drifted into sleep under the canopy of a starlit sky, dreaming of the timeless landscapes that awaited their footsteps.

Chapter 9

ANAHATA CHAKRA
(HEART CHAKRA)

As the first light of dawn crept over the horizon, Sudha and Aarohi emerged from their tent, greeted by the crisp, fresh air of the Himalayas. The campsite was already buzzing with activity as trekkers prepared for the day ahead.

They booked a room to shower and freshen up and then went out to get breakfast. After packing their essentials—water, snacks, and layers of clothing—they were ready to embark on the ascent to Tungnath, the highest Shiva temple in the world.

As they ascended the well-paved path, the scenery transformed dramatically, revealing lush forests and vibrant rhododendron blooms, and Sudha began her lesson, her voice as soothing as the light around them. "Today, Aarohi, we delve into the Anahata, or the Heart Chakra. This chakra is at the very centre of our seven major chakras, nestled between the three lower physical-emotional centres and the three upper mental-spiritual ones. It acts as a bridge, a point of integration and balance."

Aarohi listened intently, absorbing every word.

"The Heart Chakra is located at the centre of the chest, not where the physical heart organ lies, but in the middle of the thoracic spine," Sudha continued, gesturing gently to her chest. "Its element is air, and its energy governs love, compassion, and beauty. It's the core of our emotional wellbeing, empathy, and ability to give and receive love."

Sudha paused, ensuring Aarohi was following. "In Sanskrit, Anahata means 'unhurt, unstruck, and unbeaten'. It symbolises a state of purity where no harm or pain has reached. This chakra is about recognising that we are part of something larger, connected to a boundless source of love."

Aarohi nodded, her eyes reflecting a deep understanding.

"The colour associated with the Heart Chakra is green, representing growth, renewal, and the life force found in nature. It's also sometimes depicted with a soft pink, symbolising love and purity."

As they climbed higher, the forest gave way to open meadows, offering breathtaking views of the snow-capped peaks surrounding them. The beauty of the landscape provided a constant source of inspiration. Sudha, with her calm and steady presence, encouraged Aarohi, reminding her to breathe deeply and move at her own pace.

Aarohi suggested they pause for a break. They found a large boulder to sit on. Resting there, with the world spread out before them, there was a unique sense of peace, as if time itself had paused to embrace the beauty of the moment. Aarohi asked Sudha to show her the chart of Anahata Chakra. It looked like this:

Gland	Thymus
Element	Air
Location	Centre of chest
Colour	Green
Deity	Narayana and Vishnu
Animal Totem	Eagle
No. of Petals	12
Celestial body *(Graha)*	Mercury
Seed Syllable *(Beej Mantra)*	*Yam*
Organs	Heart, lungs, chest, upper back.

(Contd.,)

Sense	Touch
Food	Green vegetables

Table 5: Anahata Chakra

Pointing at the chart, Sudha started explaining, "The gland associated with the Heart Chakra is the thymus gland, which is located in the chest between the lungs. The thymus gland is most active during childhood and adolescence and plays a crucial role in the development and maturation of T-cells. T-cells, a vital component of the immune system, are a type of white blood cells."

"Does it mean that our Heart Chakra affects our immunity and vice versa?" Aarohi asked.

"Yes, that's correct," Sudha replied and continued, "Heart Chakra majorly revolves around love, forgiveness, and happiness. Talking about forgiveness reminds me of how Jesus forgave those who crucified him. He understood that they didn't really grasp the gravity of their actions. It's a bit like that for us too. Not all people are at the same point in their spiritual journey as we might be. It's like they're still waking up to a deeper understanding of life. And you know, if you find yourself on this path at a young age, it's often a sign that you're continuing something you started in a past life."

"It's really difficult to forgive someone when we know that they have intentionally tried to hurt us. It requires a different level of maturity, doesn't it?" Aarohi asked. The teacher nodded in agreement as they left the comfort of their resting spot and resumed their trek.

"The Heart Chakra, being associated with love and compassion, is like a bridge from just 'being a human' to 'being humane'," Sudha continued. "It invites individuals to move beyond the self-centred aspects of mere existence. It encourages a broader perspective that includes empathy for others, fostering a sense of interconnectedness. To fully embrace this, we need to rid ourselves of negativity."

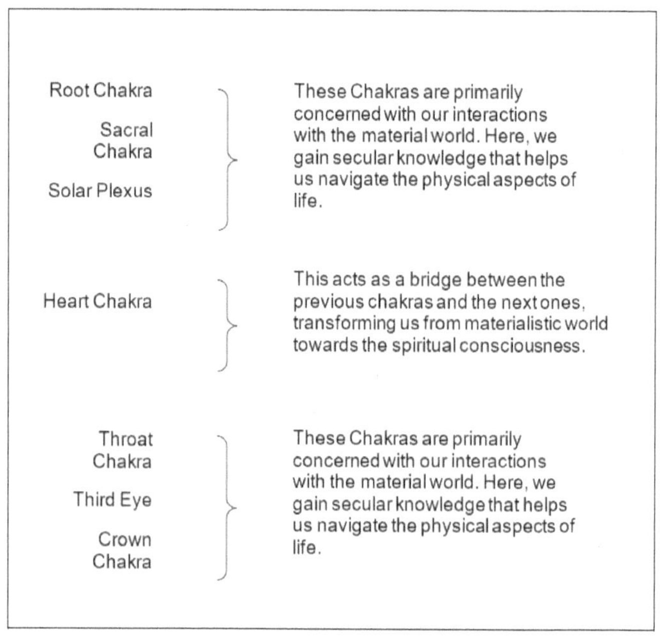

The wise lady elaborated, "When our thoughts don't mature, negativity can take over. To fix this, we need mature thoughts that bring in positivity. Think of your mind like a superhero against negativity. If your thoughts are positive, your mind can handle and fix the bad stuff in your body. So, to make your mind strong, make sure your thoughts are mature. Otherwise, the negative feelings will be hard to avoid."

"For being happy, we must focus on positivity. But it is hard to be consistently happy, especially with life's ups and downs," Aarohi reflected.

"It is," Sudha agreed, "which is why it's important to stay balanced - not just in tough times, but also when things are going great. Getting too carried away with excitement can lead to disappointment. We should find happiness in the moment, regardless of whether we get what we want or not. And it's crucial not to tie our happiness to just material things. This chakra teaches us to experience life fully but remain emotionally stable."

"But sometimes people around us do things that make us unhappy or angry," Aarohi expressed her concern.

"Other people and their actions are not in our control. Remember the lesson we learned in Manipura Chakra? To let go of things we can't control and focus on what we can control. In such situations, we can change and control ourselves, so we should focus on that," Sudha explained.

She added, her voice calm and clear, "But remember, Aarohi, it's essential not to change our core selves just to maintain harmony in our relationships. We must take responsibility for our changes and not place blame on others. Let me clarify with an example:

Suppose you have a friend who comments that you talk a lot, and you choose to speak less because of that remark. If talking is a part of who you are, suppressing this trait might lead you to feel resentment towards your friend. You might start blaming them for making you change. But it's crucial to recognise that the decision to change was yours. Others might influence us, but ultimately, we hold the power to make decisions about our behaviour."

Sudha paused to let her words sink in, then added, "Others' actions are their own karma. If someone does something wrong to you, don't let it change who you are. If you decide to change, do it because it feels right for you, not just to please or appease someone else. And if you do make that change, own it, accept it without annoyance or bitterness because the decision to change was yours. There should be no inner conflict due to such situations. This way, you maintain your emotional integrity and keep your Heart Chakra open and balanced."

Aarohi listened, the complexity of managing interpersonal relationships becoming clearer. She appreciated the practical nature of Sudha's example, realising the importance of self-awareness and personal responsibility in cultivating lasting happiness and stability. She reflected, "You mentioned that Heart Chakra also revolves around happiness. It reminded me of the time when I got my first job. I was really very happy and excited, but one of my uncles said that the pay is not that great. That statement just took away my happiness, and I started feeling sad. I wondered why someone else's opinion was bothering me and tried to get over it, but I couldn't help it."

Sudha emphasised, "Your happiness is not a visa that requires someone's stamp of approval."

She paused for a moment before resuming, "At times, we may feel sad when our happiness isn't acknowledged by others. But it's very important to remember that our happiness doesn't need someone else's approval. Your happiness is truly yours."

"I will always remember this statement," the student replied.

Sudha smiled and continued, "Our goal should be to do good, to save ourselves from negative actions and thoughts. This means not expecting too much from others and not complaining when they don't meet our expectations."

"There's so much out there that can bring us joy and satisfaction. We should try to understand others, put ourselves in their shoes, rather than expecting everyone to just listen to us," Aarohi reflected.

Sudha replied, "Exactly! The animal totem of this chakra also teaches us a good lesson. Eagles soar with extreme stability high in the sky, above the clouds, remaining untouched by rain or storms. This teaches us to stay stable, unaffected, and unharmed by difficult situations. Additionally, the eagle is the bird upon which Lord Vishnu rides."

She then added, "And there's another aspect of the Heart Chakra that directly influences our connections—the sense of touch. It plays a crucial role in how we connect and empathise with others. A simple touch or hug can make a person feel better, especially when someone is feeling sad or lonely."

"Can you tell me the emotions associated with the Heart Chakra and what do its 12 petals signify?" asked the learner.

Sudha nodded, pleased with Aarohi's eagerness to delve deeper into the teachings of the Heart Chakra. She responded warmly, "Absolutely, the emotions tied to the Heart Chakra are fundamental to understanding its influence on our lives. These include:"

EMOTIONS ASSOCIATED WITH ANAHATA CHAKRA:

- Love

- Joy

- Inner peace

- Compassion

- Empathy

- Forgiveness

She continued, "Now, regarding the twelve petals of the Heart Chakra, each symbolises a vital quality that enhances our spiritual growth. They represent:"

PETALS OF ANAHATA CHAKRA:

- Bliss

- Peace

- Harmony

- Love

- Understanding

- Empathy

- Clarity

- Purity

- Compassion

- Kindness

- Forgiveness

- Unity

"Understanding these emotions and qualities is crucial because when the Heart Chakra is blocked, it can significantly impact these areas."

"How can we tell if the Heart Chakra is blocked? What does it feel like?" asked Aarohi, intrigued.

Sudha, recognising the importance of the question, began, "When your Heart Chakra is blocked, it affects your emotions in a few ways. Let's break it down into points:

INDICATORS OF AN IMBALANCED ANAHATA CHAKRA:

- Afraid of Commitment:

  If you've been hurt before, you might try to protect yourself by avoiding commitment. For instance, if you've experienced rejection, you might shy away from new relationships or from deepening current ones to protect yourself. However, real growth and strength lie in facing these fears, not in avoiding them.

- Lack of Self-Love and Compassion:

  If the Heart Chakra is not balanced, there is a lack of self-love and compassion. It's important to accept yourself, along with your mistakes. Instead of feeling guilty about things you've done wrong, try to learn from them and make positive changes. Feeling bad about yourself doesn't help, but loving and understanding yourself does.

♦ Difficulty in Giving and Receiving Love:

Another sign of a blockage is finding it difficult to give and receive love. If you want love, you have to give it too. It's like a two-way street. Being kind and positive attracts the same back to you. You shouldn't be selfish, but you also need to take care of yourself. Staying calm, peaceful, and kind, even when things are chaotic, is the key to balance the Heart Chakra.

♦ Holding Grudges:

Grudges make it difficult to heal and fill your mind with bias. Using a gratitude journal can help with this. Being thankful, even to those who have hurt you, can be powerful and can change your perspective.

For example, if someone hurts you, thanking them might sound weird, but it helps you let go of negative feelings. If you are trapped in trouble, just remember that difficult times are an indication that good times are near. Just remember that the dawn breaks just after the darkest hour."

Aarohi listened attentively, reflecting on Sudha's explanation. She could see parallels in her own life, where she had occasionally felt the weight of these blockages.

"Thank you, Ma'am, that makes a lot of sense," Aarohi responded, a note of realisation in her voice. "I've noticed times when I've held back in relationships or have been hard on myself. It's enlightening to understand that these are signs of a blocked Heart Chakra." She paused, taking a moment to connect the dots between her experiences and Sudha's teachings. Eager to learn more about the positive aspects and how to cultivate them, Aarohi then asked, "So, how does it feel when the Heart Chakra is open? What changes might I notice in my emotions and interactions with others?"

Sudha's eyes lit up as she detailed the signs of a balanced Heart Chakra, her voice filled with encouragement. "When the Heart Chakra is open and balanced, you'll feel a significant shift in your life. It includes:"

INDICATORS OF A BALANCED ANAHATA CHAKRA:

♦ Feeling Comfortable in Relationships:

It's important to feel at ease in your relationships. This means you can both give and receive love without difficulty. Being comfortable with others helps build strong and healthy connections.

♦ Ease in Sharing and Receiving Love:

You'll also experience an ease in sharing and receiving love. This isn't just romantic love, but all forms of affection and kindness. It's a sign of a fulfilling life where relationships are built on mutual respect, care, and understanding.

♦ Gratitude for Your Life:

An open heart also brings gratitude for your life. Many people in the world struggle to have their basic needs met. If you're in a position where your essential needs are covered and you have more than the basics, it's important to be grateful. This doesn't mean you shouldn't aspire to achieve more or be inspired by those who have achieved success. However, it's crucial to appreciate what you already have while you work towards your goals.

♦ Appreciating Others and Having Compassion:

Having an open Heart Chakra enhances your ability to appreciate yourself and others and to show compassion. It's about truly empathising with others, which means understanding and sharing the feelings of others without judgement, rather than being sympathetic, which can sometimes imply feeling sorry for them. Empathy leads to healthy support and assistance, whereas sympathy can sometimes create a sense of inequality or pity.

Aarohi's face reflected a mixture of awe and introspection as she absorbed Sudha's explanation. "That sounds incredibly uplifting," she responded, her voice tinged with hope and curiosity. "To feel that level of comfort and gratitude in life... it must really change how you see the world and interact with others." She paused, clearly inspired by the idea of such emotional freedom and depth. "What can I do to help balance my Heart Chakra?"

"Balancing the Heart Chakra involves a variety of activities that focus on nurturing our emotional and physical wellbeing. Let me tell you about these practices:"

ACTIVITIES TO BALANCE ANAHATA CHAKRA:

♦ Deep Breathing:

Given that air is the fundamental element of the Heart Chakra and the lungs are its primary organs, engaging in deep breathing exercises is crucial. By inhaling deeply, we introduce more oxygen into our bodies, which aids in balancing this chakra.

♦ *Anulom Vilom*:

This is a specific type of breathing exercise that helps in regulating the flow of energy within the Heart Chakra.

♦ Receiving a Massage:

Touch is a powerful medium for energy transfer. Receiving a massage from someone who is positive and happy can transfer their positive energy to you.

♦ Self-Gratitude:

It's important to recognise and appreciate our own abilities and qualities. Loving and valuing ourselves is a stepping stone to loving others and being loved in return. This self-appreciation fosters a balanced Heart Chakra.

♦ Eating Green Vegetables:

Green vegetables are known to boost immunity. Including them in your diet can have a positive impact on your overall wellbeing and contribute to the balance of the Heart Chakra.

♦ Cooking with Love:

The energy and intention we put into cooking can be transmitted through the food we prepare. Cooking with positive intentions and love can help in nurturing the Heart Chakra.

♦ Cobra Pose:

This yoga pose is beneficial for the Heart Chakra. While performing the cobra pose, it's recommended to exhale when going against gravity and inhale when moving with gravity. This practice aids in the flow of energy within the chakra.

♦ Affirmations:

- I give and receive love, forgiveness, and compassion effortlessly and unconditionally to myself and others.

- My heart is filled with joy and gratitude.

- I am grateful for all that I have in my life.

- I am healthy, happy, and radiant.

♦ Chanting *'Beej Mantra'* or the seed syllable *'Yam'*.

Sudha smiled, her eyes shining as she shared these transformative practices.

"These activities sound incredibly impactful," the young student remarked with a note of determination in her voice.

Sudha concluded, "A well-balanced Heart Chakra empowers us to extend compassion to others, even strangers. It enhances our ability to understand others' perspectives, to empathise by putting ourselves in their shoes, and to maintain an unbiased stance between our family and others. This balance is not only essential for our emotional health but also for our interpersonal relationships."

With new knowledge and tools at her disposal, Aarohi felt a renewed sense of excitement. She was ready to embrace the practices that would open her heart and enrich her connections with others. The path ahead was clear, and she was prepared to walk it with an open heart and an eager spirit, knowing that each step was a move towards greater harmony and inner peace. This marked the beginning of a transformative journey in her life.

Illustration 4: Bhujangasana (Cobra Pose)

Chapter 10

VISHUDDHA CHAKRA (THROAT CHAKRA)

After a few hours of trekking, the ancient Tungnath Temple emerged before Sudha and Aarohi. Positioned at an impressive altitude, the temple stood majestically against the backdrop of the rugged Himalayan peaks, its ancient stones warmed by the mid-morning sun.

The air was cooler here; the occasional gusts of wind carried the scent of flowers and incense from the temple. Sudha and Aarohi paused to take in the panoramic views around them—valleys dipped in shades of green and rugged peaks crowned with lingering snow. It was a place that effortlessly bridged the divine and the earthly, and they felt a deep sense of peace as they approached the temple gates.

Removing their shoes, they stepped onto the ancient, cool stones worn smooth by centuries of pilgrims. Inside, the temple was a haven of spiritual tranquillity. Sudha and Aarohi joined other devotees, offering their prayers and seeking blessings, their voices low and reverent amidst the soft clang of bells.

After their prayer, they found a resting spot overlooking the valley. The serene environment was perfect for contemplation and deeper discussions. Sudha, sensing the pious energy of the place, turned to Aarohi.

"In this sacred space, amidst these high vibrational energies, let's explore the Vishuddha Chakra," Sudha suggested. "Located at the throat, the Vishuddha Chakra governs our ability to communicate and express ourselves freely."

Aarohi, her spirit already uplifted by the sanctity of Tungnath, nodded eagerly, ready to absorb the teachings about communication and expression that Sudha was about to share.

Sudha continued, "We'll delve into how it influences not only how we communicate with others but also how we listen and connect. When balanced, it empowers us to speak with clarity and listen with openness."

Sudha opened the chart of the Throat Chakra and started explaining.

Gland	Thyroid
Element	Space
Location	Throat
Colour	Blue
Deity	Saraswati
Animal Totem	–
No. of Petals	16
Celestial body *(Graha)*	Jupiter
Seed Syllable *(Beej Mantra)*	*Ham*
Organs	Throat, Vocal cords, jaw, mouth, neck.
Sense	Hearing
Food	Fruits, juices, and tea

Table 6: Vishuddha Chakra

"The thyroid gland, located in the front of the neck below Adam's apple, is shaped like a butterfly. It is a vital organ for metabolism, regulating it through the production of thyroid hormones, which are synthesised using iodine obtained from our diet. The gland works in coordination with the brain, particularly the hypothalamus and the pituitary gland, to maintain hormonal balance. Balancing Vishuddhi Chakra can heal thyroid disorders like hyperthyroidism and hypothyroidism."

Aarohi nodded thoughtfully, "It really shows how our physical health is connected to our spiritual state and how balancing our chakras can have a real impact on our wellbeing."

"Exactly, Aarohi. And this connection extends to how we communicate," Sudha began, explaining how the Throat Chakra symbolises clear, articulate communication. "Our words reflect our understanding and thought processes. If our understanding is clouded, our words may fail to convince others due to an inability to express our thoughts.

When we advise on something we've actually experienced ourselves, our explanations and words usually sound more convincing. This is because we can easily formulate sentences to describe real experiences, which help us give better, more relatable examples. Our way of speaking also sounds more genuine and sure.

For example, consider a salesperson recommending a specific brand of running shoes. If he hasn't worn them himself, his pitch might not sound very convincing. He might struggle to answer specific questions about comfort or performance simply because he lacks personal experience with the product.

On the other hand, when we talk about something we have used and know well, it's easier for us to think of good examples, and our words sound more convincing. This makes people more likely to believe and follow our advice because it's based on what we've really gone through, not just what we've heard from others.

Similarly, when we communicate with others, they can usually sense whether we are genuinely convinced and passionate about what we're saying. This perception is not just based on our words but also on how we say them. Our tone of voice, facial expressions, and even the level of eye contact contribute to conveying our true feelings.

For instance, consider the dynamic between a teacher and a student. Teachers are often experts at noticing when a student's attention is drifting away from the lesson. This keen observation is primarily due to the non-verbal cues or body language exhibited by the student. When someone's mind is elsewhere, their body language often reveals it. So, we communicate not just through words, but also through our body language, tone, and inflection.

If we are enthusiastic and believe in what we're discussing, our excitement and conviction are often evident, making our communication more effective. On the other hand, if we lack belief in our words, that uncertainty can also be noticed, which might make our audience sceptical as well.

Just as a student's distraction becomes apparent to a teacher, our inner conviction (or lack thereof) in our statements is often noticeable to those we communicate with. This understanding highlights the importance of congruence between our words and beliefs for effective communication."

"Oh, I never noticed how we also communicate through our body language," remarked Aarohi as they got up to resume their journey.

Rising from their reflective pause at Tungnath, Sudha and Aarohi now started heading towards the summit of

Chandrashila Peak. Under the watchful eyes of the vast Himalayan sky, they continued exploring the depths of the Vishuddha Chakra.

Sudha continued, "The Throat Chakra is also the channel through which emotions - anger, hurt, or love - are expressed. If we express these feelings through shouting in anger or suppressing them, it can create strain in the throat.

When we are clear and convinced about our feelings, our expression becomes fluent. This fluency is a sign of a balanced or open Throat Chakra.

On the other hand, if we are not transparent or honest with our emotions, it is believed that this can lead to a blockage in the Throat Chakra, making it challenging to communicate our true feelings effectively. This concept underscores the importance of authenticity in our expression.

Moreover, the Throat Chakra is considered to play a significant role in the success or failure of one's career. This is because careers often depend heavily on communication skills, whether it's speaking, listening, or expressing ideas clearly. An open and balanced Throat Chakra is thought to facilitate better communication, thereby positively influencing career success. This perspective highlights the interconnectedness of our emotional wellbeing and professional life."

"I can very much relate to it," Aarohi said thoughtfully. She paused, gathering her thoughts before continuing, "In my situation, I'm honest with my emotions, but sometimes I hesitate to speak up because I'm afraid of hurting others.

For instance, if a colleague makes a mistake, I find it difficult to call them out as I fear hurting them."

Sudha responded with understanding, "That's precisely the art of effective communication. It's something we can learn from diplomats—how to express our views while maintaining harmony in relationships. It's about expressing yourself clearly and considerately, ensuring your words build bridges rather than barriers.

When a colleague makes a mistake and you need to address it, it's best to handle the situation gently and privately. Find a quiet place where you can talk without others listening. When you talk to them, keep your voice calm and explain what went wrong clearly. Make sure to focus on the issue, not the person, so they don't feel like you're attacking them.

Ask them to share their side of the story too. This can help you both understand the situation better and think of ways to fix it. Encourage a positive approach, focusing on how to prevent the mistake in the future rather than blaming them.

Lastly, offer your help to improve things moving forward. This shows you are on their side and you care about making things better together. This way, you can help fix the mistake and also strengthen your working relationship."

"That makes a lot of sense," Aarohi said enthusiastically. "I can see how this approach not only solves the problem but also builds trust and strengthens relationships at work. I'll definitely keep this in mind for the future. Thank you for the guidance."

Sudha smiled, pleased with Aarohi's receptiveness, and continued to elaborate on the complexities of the Throat Chakra. "The Throat Chakra is linked with the sense of hearing. This connection emphasises the importance of listening," she explained. "True communication involves listening just as much as it does speaking. By fully hearing others, we engage more deeply, understanding their perspectives and feelings which, in turn, enhances our own responses and expressions."

She paused to ensure Aarohi grasped the full implications. "This also allows for a richer, more meaningful exchange of ideas, fostering stronger relationships and better problem-solving abilities. It's about creating a balance between expressing your own voice and being open to the voices of others.

Additionally, this highlights the idea that clarity in listening to our inner voice enhances the clarity with which others understand our spoken words. It represents the deep interconnection between self-awareness and how we express ourselves to the world."

Aarohi nodded thoughtfully, recalling a relevant quote that underscored Sudha's point. "It reminds me of a saying I once heard," she mentioned, "It goes, 'The biggest communication problem is we do not listen to understand, we listen to reply.' It really highlights how listening should be about understanding the other person's perspective, not just preparing what to say next."

Sudha nodded in agreement. As they progressed, the trail gradually transformed, becoming steeper and more challenging. The teacher continued her lesson, "Talking about the symbol of Throat Chakra, it is represented by blue colour and has 16 petals which represent the following:"

PETALS OF VISHUDDHA CHAKRA:

♦ Seven musical notes:

   Seven petals of this chakra represent the seven musical notes, called *'swaras'* in traditional Indian music and commonly represented using the seven notes: *Sa, Re, Ga, Ma, Pa, Dha,* and *Ni.*

♦ Five Elements of Nature:

   The next five petals of the Throat Chakra represent the five elements of nature, namely earth, water, fire, air, and space.

♦ Preface.

♦ Context

♦ Conclusion.

♦ Immortality

"Preface, context, and conclusion are integral parts of speech. We know that people are remembered by their words; our words live on even after we're gone, keeping our ideas and values alive. This way, words can make us immortal, as they continue to influence others even after our death."

Aarohi nodded as she grasped the immense power of words. Sudha then moved ahead with the lesson, sharing the key emotions tied to the Throat Chakra.

EMOTIONS ASSOCIATED WITH VISHUDDHA CHAKRA:

"This chakra is centrally concerned with:

- Self-expression.

- Communication

- Finding your authentic voice

- Speaking the truth"

"Could you explain all the consequences of the blocked Throat Chakra?" Aarohi inquired, eager to grasp the full implications.

Sudha began, "Certainly! If the Throat Chakra is blocked, you experience the following:"

INDICATORS OF AN IMBALANCED VISHUDDHA CHAKRA:

♦ You are afraid to speak what you feel.

   You might find yourself holding back your true feelings or desires. It's like having the right thoughts, but a hesitance in expressing them. This hesitation could stem from a lack of conviction in your beliefs or a lack of confidence in articulating them. It's essential to understand that your voice and your truth have immense value.

♦ You go along with others so you don't upset anyone:

   If your Throat Chakra is blocked, you may often agree with others, even if you don't share the same views. This tendency to fit in is usually driven by a desire to avoid conflict or displeasure. However, remember that your opinions are as significant as anyone else's. It's about striking a balance between harmony with others and authenticity in your expressions.

♦ You feel a sore throat frequently.

Physical manifestations like frequent sore throat, neck pain, or thyroid issues can also be signs of a blocked Throat Chakra. It symbolises the suppressed words and emotions that struggle to find a voice.

INDICATORS OF A BALANCED VISHUDDHA CHAKRA:

"On the flip side, when this chakra is open and balanced, the transformation is radical.

- You are comfortable speaking your truth.

- You experience others listening to you.

- You feel that you are heard and honoured for your truth.

You'll find yourself confidently expressing your truth, and doing so brings you a sense of liberation and authenticity. You'll notice that others listen to you more attentively, respecting and valuing your viewpoints. This respect is not just about agreement; it's about acknowledging the validity and worth of your perspective. When you speak, your words carry weight and sincerity, earning you a reputation for honesty and integrity. People start to believe in your words, recognising the wisdom and truth you bring to the conversation."

Having realised that she needs to balance this chakra, Aarohi was eager to know how she could work towards healing it. Sensing her determination, Sudha offered a variety of practical exercises and activities designed to open and balance the Throat Chakra. "Here are some activities to maintain balance in your Throat Chakra:

ACTIVITIES TO BALANCE VISHUDDHA CHAKRA:

- Reading out loud:

  Practising this helps you hear your own pitch and tone, allowing you to make adjustments and become more confident in your voice.

- Chanting "*Om*" seven times:

  This helps in sound healing. It vibrates at the frequency of the Throat Chakra, promoting energy flow and healing.

- Recording and listening to your own voice:

  This exercise can greatly improve your speaking skills by making you more aware of how you sound and how you express yourself.

- Speaking while looking at yourself in the mirror:

  This helps you observe and evaluate your body language and facial expressions, which are key components of effective communication.

- Singing and chanting:

  Singing and chanting are excellent for expressing yourself freely and creatively, which stimulates the Throat Chakra.

- Shoulder stand:

  A yoga pose that is particularly effective for stimulating the Throat Chakra, helping to promote better energy flow through this area.

- ♦ Consuming fruits, juices, and tea:

  These are gentle on the throat and can help cleanse the Throat Chakra, fostering better health.

- ♦ Rolling your neck:

  This simple physical exercise helps in releasing any tension held in the throat area.

- ♦ Saying these affirmations:

  - I communicate with clarity.

  - I speak my truth.

  - I choose positive self-talk.

  - I express myself with creativity.

  - I express what I feel with strength, confidence, and honesty.

  - I listen intently when others are speaking.

- ♦ Chanting the *'Beej mantra'* or seed syllable *'Ham'*.

- ♦ Journaling:

  If there is nobody to share your feelings with, you can also opt for journaling. It's an excellent tool for listening to yourself."

Illustration 5: Sarvangasana (Shoulderstand)

Sudha emphasised the importance of regular practice and consistency with these techniques to effectively heal and maintain a balanced Throat Chakra.

Aarohi pondered over the points Sudha had outlined, then voiced a realisation. "Self-confidence is crucial to be able to express ourselves without hesitation, so there seems to be a relation between the Solar Plexus and the Throat Chakra."

Pleased with Aarohi's insight, Sudha affirmed, "Yes, you're absolutely right." She continued, "In fact, the Throat, Solar Plexus, and Heart Chakras are closely intertwined in governing our emotional and expressive capacities."

RELATIONSHIP AMONG THE THROAT, SOLAR PLEXUS, AND HEART CHAKRAS:

"A blockage in the Throat Chakra can lead to feelings of being unheard or unable to express oneself. This can trigger emotional disturbances linked to the Heart Chakra, as one might feel hurt. Additionally, when one's voice feels suppressed or unvalued, it can adversely affect the Solar Plexus Chakra, leading to a loss of self-confidence. This demonstrates how the chakras interrelate and affect each other."

With each step, the significance of their discussion resonated within Aarohi, weaving through her thoughts like the path they traversed. Aarohi now understood that maintaining chakra balance was not just a practice but a lifestyle—a commitment to nurturing her entire being for holistic health and harmony.

"As we continue our climb," Sudha said, her voice steady against the crisp mountain air, "think of each step as a movement towards greater balance and clarity in your life. The lessons from the Throat Chakra are vital as they empower you to express your truth and to listen deeply, qualities essential for any journey, whether spiritual, personal, or professional."

Grateful for the insights and the beautiful setting in which they were shared, Aarohi felt equipped and motivated to continue her journey of self-discovery and healing. She was excited to explore and embrace her inner voice with confidence and grace.

Chapter 11

AGYA CHAKRA (THIRD EYE CHAKRA)

As the student-teacher duo continued their ascent towards Chandrashila Peak, the sun cast a golden glow across the rugged trail. Amidst the serenity of the high mountains, Sudha introduced the concept of the Third Eye Chakra to Aarohi. "Also known as the Brow Chakra, *'Agya'*, *'Ajna'*, *'Brihumadhya'*, or *'Dwidak Padam'* (the two-petalled lotus), the Third Eye Chakra is the centre of intuition, foresight, and inner wisdom."

Sudha explained, her gaze reflecting the deep blue sky, "This chakra governs our ability to see both the outer and inner worlds, blending the seen and the unseen into our sense of understanding.

The 'gut feeling' or an instinctive sense we experience is actually the voice of our inner self. It guides us through life's complexities and can help us make better decisions. Always acknowledge and trust this voice, Aarohi. It's there to show you the right direction when you face uncertainty."

"When I was younger, I was confused about what I wanted to do in life. I still sometimes do not get clarity in certain things. Is it related to an imbalanced Third Eye Chakra?" asked Aarohi.

"Yes, you're right! When the Ajna Chakra is balanced, you know what you want in life, you get quick clarity in a lot of things. You can make decisions with clarity. But don't worry, little kid, as we explore the depths of this chakra and as you start activating this chakra with the help of the activities I will mention, you will start seeing the difference." Aarohi listened intently as Sudha continued, "Many people get caught up in the materialistic world, only to realise at the end of their lives that they missed out on their true purpose.

Activation of the Third Eye Chakra, even to the slightest degree, can trigger a spiritual awakening, sparking interest in spirituality. Intuition, a key aspect of this chakra, is something everyone experiences at some point. For instance, the sudden feeling that something isn't right about a situation, even when everything appears normal, is an example of intuition at work. Activating the Third

Eye is also believed to help in balancing of other chakras, particularly when there are minor imbalances.

Regular focus and meditation on the Third Eye Chakra can improve spiritual knowledge and the ability to make foresighted decisions. If fully activated in this lifetime, it is considered a remarkable achievement. While meditating, we may get some visions. If you observe, you will notice that initially, we see them through the left eye. However, with continued practice, a more panoramic perspective emerges, including the ability to watch it through the right eye as well. This progression is particularly significant; seeing through the right eye indicates that Ajna Chakra has begun to balance."

Looking for a brief rest, the duo found a rock to sit on. Sudha pulled a small chart from her backpack, which looked as follows:

Gland	Pineal
Element	Light
Location	Centre of the forehead, Slightly above the junction of the eyebrows.
Colour	Indigo
Deity	Durga
Animal Totem	–
No. of Petals	2
Celestial body *(Graha)*	Saturn
Seed Syllable *(Beej Mantra)*	*Om*
Organs	Eyes, ears, sinuses, lower brain

(Contd.,)

Sense	Intuition (Sixth Sense)
Food	Blueberries, grapes, and dark chocolates

Table 7: Ajna Chakra

Elucidating on the relationship between the Third Eye Chakra and the pineal gland, the spiritual guide continued, "The pineal gland, reddish-grey in colour, is located in the epithalamus, near the centre of the brain, between the two hemispheres. The primary function of the pineal gland is to produce melatonin, a hormone that modulates sleep patterns. It is involved in regulating various biological rhythms, including the sleep-wake cycle. Disruptions in melatonin production or secretion can affect sleep patterns, potentially leading to insomnia."

Connecting the dots, Aarohi queried with a realisation, "Oh, so if someone is experiencing sleeplessness, it might be related to an imbalance in either the Muladhara Chakra or the Third Eye Chakra?"

"Yes, exactly!" the teacher affirmed. "In that case, we have to analyse additional symptoms to be able to identify which chakra is imbalanced."

Looking at the symbol of the Ajna Chakra, Aarohi's curiosity was piqued by its simplicity compared to other chakra symbols. "The symbol of this chakra has only two petals. What do they signify?" she asked.

PETALS OF AGYA CHAKRA:

Sudha replied warmly, "The two petals of the Ajna Chakra stand for two types of knowledge. The first, called *'Apar'*, is everyday worldly knowledge. The second, *'Par'*, means spiritual or higher knowledge that goes beyond the ordinary. *'Par'* represents moving past pain, sadness, and material concerns. It's about reaching a state of freedom from grief and pain, which we achieve after we've balanced the Heart Chakra. Hence, at this stage, there is no discussion of negativity."

Aarohi nodded thoughtfully, absorbing the depth of the explanation. "It's like reaching a point where you're not just living but understanding life at a much deeper level. No wonder the Third Eye Chakra opens you up to a different dimension of consciousness."

"What are the emotions associated with this chakra?" Aarohi asked after a pause.

Sudha's response highlighted a shift in perspective. "When an individual is successful in balancing all the five chakras preceding the Third Eye Chakra, it signifies that they have learned to manage their emotions. Therefore, the attributes linked to this chakra extend beyond emotions. These attributes include:"

ATTRIBUTES ASSOCIATED WITH AGYA CHAKRA:

- Visualisation - Not only does visualisation help balance this chakra, but activation of the Agya Chakra also enhances the ability to create vivid mental images.

- Wisdom - Activation of the Agya Chakra makes a person wise, enabling them to blend their knowledge and experience to make sound, insightful judgements and decisions. They skillfully execute what they have learned and put their knowledge into practice.

♦ Intuition - This chakra is closely tied to intuitive power, which can lead to magical transformations in our lives.

♦ Decision-Making Skills - It sharpens the ability to make swift, yet thoughtful decisions. But always remember that while we can control our choices, their outcomes often remain beyond our control.

As the wind whispered through the mountain passes, Aarohi posed another question, "What are the signs that indicate whether this chakra is blocked or open?"

Sudha stated, "When the Ajna Chakra is imbalanced, you experience the following:

INDICATORS OF AN IMBALANCED AGYA CHAKRA:

♦ You feel disconnected from your intuition or feel like you don't have any.

♦ You feel lost when it comes to your spiritual purpose and path in life.

♦ You get headaches and feel tension in your brow area.

♦ It is difficult to make decisions because of a lack of gut feeling.

On the other hand, when the Third Eye Chakra is open, it's quite transformative:

INDICATORS OF A BALANCED AGYA CHAKRA:

♦ Your intuition is your guide that you trust.

- You have a strong sense of your own inner truth and you listen to it and follow it.

- You act with confidence based on your intuition.

- You can make decisions with clarity."

Eager to activate her Third Eye Chakra, Aarohi inquired enthusiastically, "Could you guide me on how to balance this chakra?"

Sudha smiled and began explaining, "Activating the Third Eye Chakra can enable us to distinguish truth from falsehood, evaluate situations accurately, and provide insights into past or future lives. Activating this chakra provides immense swiftness in life. Let me tell you some activities to do the same:"

ACTIVITIES TO BALANCE AGYA CHAKRA:

- Visualisation:

    Visualise your goals as if they've already been achieved rather than something to be accomplished in the future. This enhances the power of the Third Eye Chakra, which in turn strengthens our self-image. Visualise in a way that you feel the emotions that you would feel after achieving your goals. These emotions help us vibrate at the frequency of our goals, which in turn helps us attract them effortlessly.

- Chanting Mantras:

    Chanting mantras can help in balancing this chakra. It can be further enhanced by visualising a deity while chanting.

- Watching the sunrise and sunset:

  Observing these natural phenomena can help in the activation of the Third Eye Chakra.

- Child's Pose:

  This yoga pose increases blood circulation to the head, which, in turn, aids in activation of this chakra.

- Affirmations: These affirmations can help in balancing this chakra:

  - I am intuitive and connected to my inner guidance.

  - I know my intuition will guide me in the right direction.

  - My imagination is vivid and powerful.

  - I always trust my intuition.

- Chanting the *'Beej Mantra'*:

  Chanting *'Om'* has numerous benefits. It not only helps in balancing this chakra but also improves focus and concentration, enhances mental alertness, etc.

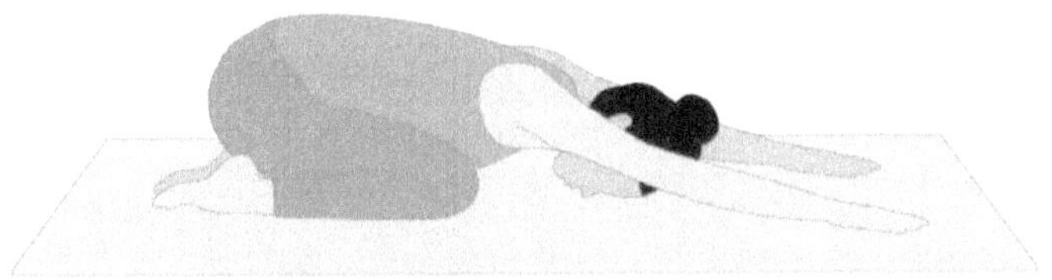

Illustration 6: Balasana (Child's Pose)

Sudha suggested they practise a short meditation to stimulate the Third Eye. "Let's use this magnificent setting to our advantage," she proposed. "The vastness around us can help dissolve the boundaries of our ordinary perception and open us up to deeper insights."

Aarohi nodded in agreement, eager to experience the practices that could awaken great abilities. As they settled into a meditative posture, focusing on the space between their eyebrows, Sudha guided Aarohi to close her eyes, relax her body and mind, and take a few deep breaths.

She then asked her to clearly define what she wanted to achieve. Whether it's a career goal, the activation of a chakra, or simply a state of being, knowing exactly what we want to focus on is very crucial. In her soothing voice, Sudha guided, "Try to use all your senses to make the visualisation as vivid as possible. Imagine not just how things look, but also how they feel, sound, smell, and even taste. The more detailed your visualisation, the more effective it will be. Now feel that you have already achieved your goal; try to feel exactly how you would feel upon achieving it. Experience that feeling right now. Joy, excitement, peace—feel these emotions deeply."

Their meditation deepened, accompanied by the rhythmic sounds of nature and the gentle caress of the afternoon breeze. After a while, Sudha, in her soft voice, instructed Aarohi to slowly rub her palms together and place them over her eyes before opening them. Aarohi followed her guidance and slowly opened her eyes, feeling an overwhelming sense of calm and connection to her inner self and the world around her.

As they sat there for a while longer, soaking in the peace of the moment and the beauty of their surroundings, Aarohi felt gratitude for the experience and for Sudha's guidance.

Eventually, they gathered themselves, their spirits lifted and minds clear, ready to resume their trek. As they continued their journey, with renewed energy, Sudha concluded, "Like any skill, visualisation gets better with practice. Regular sessions, even short ones, can greatly improve your ability to create clear and effective mental images. In essence, the Third Eye Chakra connects us to the supreme element, enhancing gut feelings, practicality, and our inner voice. By attaining a higher level of purity of intentions along with emotional stability, we can become more connected to divine power."

As they wrapped up their deep dive into the Third Eye Chakra, Aarohi experienced a deep sense of comprehension. The chakra's association with intuitive decision-making and visualisation resonated deeply with her. She now saw how enhancing these aspects could lead her towards a more fulfilling life. Excited by Sudha's suggestion of visualisation exercises and chanting mantras, Aarohi was eager to integrate these practices into her daily routine. With a sense of gratitude and anticipation, she thanked Sudha for another enriching conversation, looking forward to their continued exploration of the chakras. The divine power of the Third Eye Chakra lingered in their minds, symbolising a higher level of purity that goes beyond emotional influence and connects us to a supreme power.

Chapter 12

SAHASRARA CHAKRA (CROWN CHAKRA)

Finally, after an insightful journey, Sudha and Aarohi reached the peak of Chandrashila. As they stood at the summit, they were greeted with a panoramic view that took their breath away. The vast expanse of the Himalayas stretched before them, the snow-capped peaks bathed in the golden light of the afternoon sun, casting a serene glow over the rugged landscape. They took a moment to absorb the majesty of nature, feeling a great sense of achievement and peace.

The quietness at the top, with only the occasional sound of the wind, made the moment feel even more magical, as if they were outside of regular time. The tranquil environment and stunning view were perfect for them to reflect and feel even more connected to nature.

After their silent admiration, Sudha and Aarohi were ready to discuss the final and most sublime of the chakras. "We've reached not just the physical peak of Chandrashila but also an ideal place to explore the peak of our spiritual journey through the chakras—the Sahasrara or Crown Chakra," Sudha began, her voice blending with the gentle wind.

"Located at the top of the head, it's often shown as emitting a divine light that goes beyond the physical world. This chakra symbolises the peak of spiritual progress, where we reach a state of pure awareness and oneness with the universe," Sudha explained as she opened the chart of the Crown Chakra.

Gland	Pituitary
Element	Thought (Beyond the worldly elements)
Location	Top of the head

(Contd.,)

Colour	Violet
Deity	Shiva
Animal Totem	—
No. of Petals	1000 and more
Celestial body *(Graha)*	*'Rahu'*
Seed Syllable *(Beej Mantra)*	*Om*
Organs	Cerebrum, Hypothalamus
Sense	Thought
Food	—

Table 8: Sahasrara Chakra

Aarohi listened intently as Sudha continued, "The word 'Sahasrara' translates to 'thousand-petalled,' symbolising the infinite nature of this chakra. It's not just a symbolic entity but a vibrant vortex of energy, acting as the gateway to higher states of being and spiritual growth. Its role is crucial because it represents the final stage of energy ascent, where our personal consciousness blends with the universal."

Aarohi's eyes lit up. "It sounds like the point where everything comes together, where our inner self connects with something much larger than us."

Sudha smiled in agreement and elaborated, "The Crown Chakra acts as a channel for both inner and outer beauty. Inner beauty is about the purity and clarity of a person's spirit, while outer beauty is about the personality that others can see. This chakra deepens our connection with the divine, improving our aura and personality so much that others are naturally drawn to us. Your wisdom, intellect, mindfulness, and memory go beyond the finest; your ability to listen becomes exceptionally strong. You become a charismatic leader with speech that feels like nectar dripping from your mouth."

Aarohi's eyes widened with a mix of awe and curiosity, her mind racing with the implications. "So, by activating this chakra, we're not just improving ourselves; we're also radiating that positive energy outward, affecting those around us."

"Precisely," Sudha continued. "Activating the Crown Chakra leads to greater independence and a move beyond just physical existence, often described as becoming a 'child of God'."

She continued, "The Crown Chakra helps us overcome biases and earthly attachments. We get thoughts out of this earth, about expansive concepts like the universe, time, and space. This chakra allows us to feel that we are a part of the universal flow and bestows a sense of blessedness. We feel such satisfaction and fulfilment that it makes us feel as if there's heaven on earth."

Aarohi added, "It feels like it could take several lifetimes to achieve this state of being."

Sudha exclaimed, "That's actually true, but when reached, it can be described as a state of bliss. It's a state where our intentions towards others are at their purest, and we can't think ill of anyone. We are at a super conscious level where we are aware of our feelings and instinctively understand and assess situations with clarity and wisdom.

The power of this chakra can manifest in a simple smile that radiates a hundred words, signifying the potency of one's aura. Activation of this chakra suggests a balance or alignment across all chakras, which in turn implies mental and physical fitness."

Aarohi nodded. She paused thoughtfully before responding, "That sounds incredibly powerful. To think that such a state of bliss and deep connection could be achieved... It makes the spiritual journey seem so worthwhile. It's almost like reaching a state of enlightenment where everything in life aligns perfectly." Her voice carried a mix of reverence and a newly sparked determination to pursue this path further. "How does it feel when this chakra is blocked?" she asked.

Sudha smiled and explained, "When Sahasrara Chakra is blocked, you feel the following:"

INDICATORS OF AN IMBALANCED SAHASRARA CHAKRA:

- Lack of focus.

- You feel no connection or guidance with a supreme power or higher power.

- You feel unworthy of spiritual help and feel angry that your higher power has abandoned you.

- You suffer from migraines.

"Blockages in the Crown Chakra can result in feeling disconnected from or abandoned by a higher power, leading to feelings of unworthiness and anger. Those with a blocked Crown Chakra often struggle to understand their life's purpose, so they often blame others for their discontent."

Aarohi's expression grew more serious as she thought about the times she felt the same. "How does it feel when this chakra is balanced?" she asked.

Sudha answered, "When this chakra is balanced, you experience:"

INDICATORS OF A BALANCED SAHASRARA CHAKRA:

♦   Connection to a higher power.

♦   You know you deserve immense blessings.

♦   You feel universal love and appreciation for yourself and others, and you are grateful for these feelings.

♦   All your senses are under your control.

"When the Crown Chakra is open, there's an immense feeling of connection to a higher power. You feel that the almighty is with you and you embrace the principles of *karma*. You are grateful for everything that you have received in your life. You appreciate others' achievements and express genuine happiness for them. This sense of reverence and gratitude can only be truly experienced with an open Crown Chakra."

Aarohi's face relaxed into a gentle serenity as she imagined the peace that an open Crown Chakra might bring. "It sounds so beautiful, like everything would just... click into place. I'd love to reach that state of being."

"It's a state worth striving for," Sudha agreed, her voice filled with warmth and hope. As they sat at the peak, enveloped by the vast sky and the ethereal beauty of the mountains, the setting seemed perfectly attuned for discussing such spiritual truths. "What do the petals of Sahasrara Chakra symbolise?" asked Aarohi eagerly.

PETALS OF SAHASRARA CHAKRA:

"The petals of the Crown Chakra symbolise all the feelings and emotions a human can experience. It includes all those feelings that we have discussed in previous lessons and more, not limited to a thousand. To activate the Crown Chakra, one should have control over their emotions. One should not be ruled by their emotions. Our emotions should guide us, but not control us."

Aarohi's eyes widened with realisation as she absorbed Sudha's words. The idea that emotions, which she often felt so intensely, were not meant to control her but to guide her to know herself better, struck a deep chord within her. She nodded slowly, her mind racing to connect this understanding with her own experiences. A sense of calm washed over her as she began to see the path to mastering her emotions, and with it, the possibility of unlocking the potential of the Crown Chakra.

"That makes so much sense," she whispered, her voice filled with a mix of awe and determination. "Can you tell me the ways to balance the Crown Chakra?" asked Aarohi with anticipation.

Sudha responded enthusiastically, "Activities to balance Crown Chakra include:"

ACTIVITIES TO BALANCE SAHASRARA CHAKRA:

- Performing the Headstand pose.

- Performing Surya Namaskar.

- Rolling your head.

- Fasting.

- Regular meditation and prayer.

- Practising *'Pranayama'* or breath control exercises. These improve oxygen intake, enhancing gland functionality.

- Engaging in cardiovascular exercises.

- Breathing fresh air and watching the sunrise.

- Affirmations:

  - I am complete and one with the Divine energy.

  - I am light. I am love.

  - I am connected to the universe.

  - The universe supports and guides me.

- Chanting *'Beej Mantra'* or seed syllable *'Om'*.

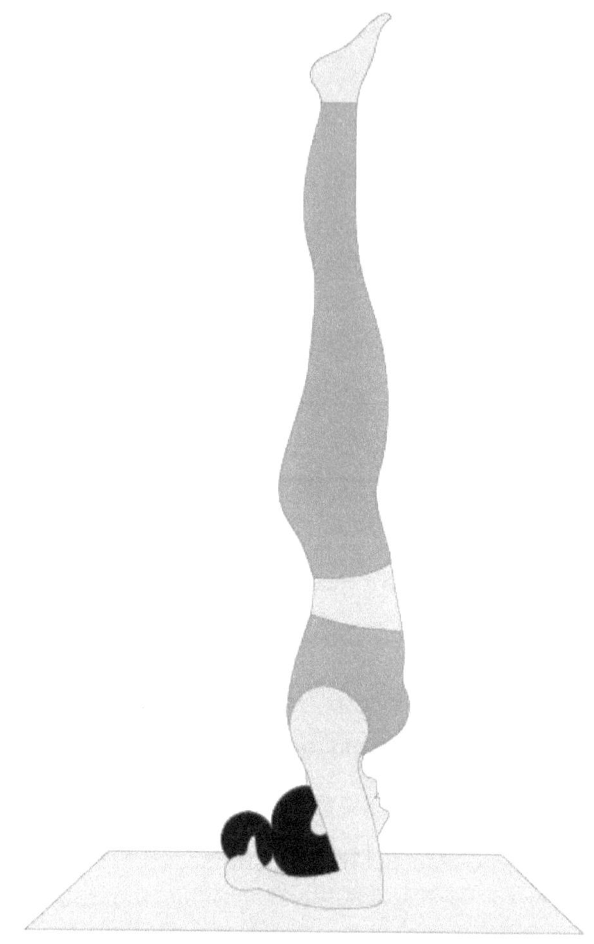

Illustration 7: Shirshasana (Headstand)

Aarohi chuckled lightly. "The Headstand pose might be a bit tricky for me," Sudha chuckled along with her. "It's understandable, and it's always important to practise such poses under the guidance of an expert."

The student nodded in agreement. Sudha then delved deeper into the significance of balancing the Sahasrara Chakra. "In Hinduism, Goddess Parvati symbolises power or '*Shakti*'. She is the consort of Shiva, the supreme deity or the God of Gods. To form a connection with the divine power—Shiva, we must fully activate our '*Shakti*'. This leads to the union of our soul with the supreme soul—God.

Activating our power to the fullest potential happens when all the chakras are activated. So this union of 'power of self' with the 'Divine Energy' occurs when all our chakras are activated, when the Crown Chakra is activated."

Aarohi absorbed Sudha's explanation with keen interest, the nature of the teachings resonating deeply within her. "That's incredibly powerful," she responded thoughtfully. "The idea that activating our Crown Chakra can lead to a union with the divine really emphasises the spiritual significance of our journey through the chakras."

She paused, reflecting on the connection between the physical practices and the spiritual outcomes they were aiming for. "It's like each step we take in balancing our chakras brings us closer not just to personal health and harmony, but to a deeper, spiritual relationship with the universe."

Sudha smiled, pleased with Aarohi's understanding and engagement. "Exactly," she affirmed. "Our spiritual journey is about aligning our inner energy with the universal energy. It's a beautiful path of growth, discovery, and connection."

Aarohi felt a deep sense of fulfilment and gratitude. Each chakra, from the root to the crown, had taught her something unique about herself, the world around, and her place in the universe.

As she stood there, the cool wind whispering around her, Aarohi realised that the end of these lessons was not just a conclusion but a new beginning. Armed with this knowledge, she was now equipped to continue her spiritual growth independently, applying what she had learned to achieve balance, harmony, and deeper spiritual connections.

Turning to Sudha, Aarohi expressed her heartfelt thanks. "This journey has been truly enlightening, and I feel ready to embrace whatever comes next with an open heart and a clear mind. Thank you for guiding me through this."

Sudha smiled warmly, acknowledging the significant strides Aarohi had made. "Remember, the learning never really ends," she advised. "Keep exploring, keep balancing, and keep connecting with your chakras. They are the key to maintaining your spiritual, emotional, and physical wellbeing."

Aarohi was now more committed than ever to continue her practice, motivated by the possibility of achieving such a transformative spiritual connection. She felt inspired and rejuvenated, ready to face life's challenges with fresh strength and wisdom. With a final look at the stunning view, they began their descent, each step echoing the lessons learned.

Chapter 13

ADDITIONAL TECHNIQUES TO BALANCE CHAKRAS

While they were on their descent from the majestic Chandrashila Peak, the sun was tilting towards the horizon, casting long shadows and painting the sky with hues of orange and pink. The air was tinged with the scent of pine and fresh mountain soil.

Aarohi, feeling a bit hungry yet contemplative, turned to Sudha. "I've been thinking about how diet influences our chakra balance. Could you provide some insight into how I can align my eating habits to enhance this process?"

"Indeed, Aarohi. You've touched upon a vital aspect of holistic wellbeing. Our diet greatly influences our energy levels, and by extension, the balance of our chakras. You see, our consumption patterns directly impact the flow of life force energy, or prana, within us.

Remember the proverb 'We are what we eat'. Let me guide you through some key dietary principles that can enhance your life force energy," replied Sudha and shared some important points that Aarohi listened to with keen interest:

- **Incorporate Fresh Greens:** Include a variety of fresh, green leafy vegetables like spinach in your meals as they are rich in high life force energy.

- **Choose Fresh Food:** Always opt for fresh meals to avoid the low vibrational energy of stale foods. Also, opt for fresh fruits or meals over frozen food.

- **Cooking Methods Matter:** Avoid overcooking your food and avoid chopping the vegetables too finely to retain the nutritional content.

- **Prefer Whole Fruits to Juices:** Opt for whole fruits instead of their juices as juicing often strips away fibre, reducing nutritional benefits. Also, juices have a higher Glycemic Index compared to whole fruits, leading to a potential increase in your body's sugar levels. If you prefer juices, choose unfiltered juice as it retains more fibre than filtered juice. Additionally, consume freshly extracted juices within 20 minutes to retain maximum nutrients.

- **Protein for Physical and Energetic Repair:** Include protein sources in your diet to support muscle repair and energy levels.

- **Be Cautious with Certain Food Combinations:** Be cautious with certain food combinations that may interact negatively. These include iron with calcium, milk combined with salty foods, figs, or dates, as well as sour substances like tomatoes. Additionally, avoid pairing onions with curd, fish with dairy, and black lentils (*urad dal*) with curd.

- **Incorporate *sattvic* food in diet:** Incorporate *sattvic* food, known for its high life force energy, into your diet. Try to avoid non-vegetarian food as it is often prepared with excessive spices leading to acidity. Further, the harsh treatment and negative energy associated with animal slaughtering can permeate the meat, potentially bringing aggressive tendencies in consumers. These adverse effects contradict the serenity essential for spiritual growth. Hence, it's important that our diet primarily consists of positive energy.

- It's crucial to make conscious choices during periods of extreme hunger or fatigue. Consuming junk food may provide temporary satisfaction but may later lead to guilt and health issues. Instead, opt for wholesome foods like fruits that leave you feeling refreshed and satisfied. It's not about eliminating flavourful foods, but controlling our intake for balanced energy.

Aarohi listened intently as Sudha detailed the dietary adjustments she could make to better align her chakras. As the sun dipped below the horizon, Sudha's face was softly lit by the fading light, giving her words an almost mystical weight as she emphasised the importance of life force energy in their daily meals.

As they continued their descent, Sudha introduced some more methods to balance chakras:

- Engaging in physical exercise is an essential component in the alignment of chakras. Activities such as aerobics, cardiovascular workouts, brisk walking, trekking, and forest walks encourage oxygen intake and its distribution throughout every cell of our body, thus facilitating chakra balance.

- Water, constituting approximately 60% of our bodies, is our vital power centre. It plays a crucial role in detoxification, promoting the health of our kidneys, gallbladder, and digestive system. Similarly, the earth's power centres are water bodies. Walking beside rivers, ponds, and lakes or simply enjoying the soothing sound of waves can foster mental healing.

- Receiving a massage from a cheerful and vibrant individual can positively influence your energy. Surrounding yourself with plants, which absorb negative energy, as well as aromatic elements such as roses or rose petals and Gum Benzoin or *"Loban Dhoop"*, can also contribute to a harmonious environment.

- As the ocean absorbs much of nature's negativity due to its saline water, a similar process can be applied personally. Immersing your feet in warm water with a spoonful of sea salt at night can help absorb and cleanse negative energy from your body.

- Meditating under a tree can provide a feeling of support and grounding, so hugging a tree can be an excellent method for energy exchange.

Sudha then explains grounding and its importance:

- Grounding is the process of releasing excess energy obtained during meditation. To achieve this, stand barefoot on the ground and visualise the excess energy flowing into the earth. Our bodies and the earth maintain a continuous energy exchange. Wearing footwear disrupts this flow; therefore, it is crucial to spend some time grounding each day, especially after meditation.

As they approached Chopta, the base, exhaustion faded into peaceful contentment. The journey had been physically demanding, but the emotional and spiritual rewards far outweighed any fatigue. Aarohi and Sudha found a small, cosy guesthouse to rest for the night. As they drifted into sleep, their thoughts danced with visions of a beautiful life ahead, filled with promise and endless possibilities.

The next morning, they woke with the sun, its golden rays gently nudging them back to the reality of their descent. After a simple breakfast, they packed their belongings and began their journey to Rishikesh. The drive was serene, with the early morning light casting a soft glow over the emerald green valleys and the winding Ganges River below. Aarohi felt a great sense of clarity and peace, a new hope blooming within her. The journey had sparked something deep inside her—a realisation of her purpose in life.

As they neared Rishikesh, Aarohi turned to Sudha with a question that had been on her mind since the previous night. "Ma'am, I want to ask about your fees for guiding me through this journey."

Sudha chuckled a little, her eyes reflecting the wisdom and kindness that had guided Aarohi through her transformative experience. "Aarohi, my fee is simple," she said, her voice gentle yet firm. "Promise me that you will stay strong and positive in all situations life throws at you, no matter how difficult they may seem. Face them head-on, with courage and grace. And most importantly, spread these lessons to as many people as you can. Share this knowledge, this energy, with those who need it. That will be the greatest reward you can give me."

Aarohi felt a surge of emotion, her heart swelling with gratitude. She nodded, understanding the depth of what Sudha was asking. It wasn't just a promise; it was a commitment to a new way of life, one filled with purpose and intention.

As they reached Rishikesh, it was time for them to part ways. The bond they had formed over the past few days was remarkably strong, yet both knew that this was where their paths diverged. They hugged each other tightly, their connection transcending words. With a final wave, Aarohi watched as Sudha disappeared into the bustling streets of the sacred town, leaving her with a sense of calm and determination.

Aarohi booked her flight back to Canada. As she sat by the river, waiting for her departure, she felt a deep sense of peace. Her curiosity about the mysteries of hidden supernatural powers had been satisfied, giving way to a clear vision of her future. She felt a strong urge to give as much as she could to the world. Aarohi knew that her journey wouldn't end with her return home; in fact, it was just beginning.

Her pure inner self, which had always been there, was now emerging with renewed strength. The lessons she had learned were not just for her own benefit but were meant to be shared with the world. She felt a powerful calling to give back, to spread the light and wisdom she had gained from this journey.

As the sun began to set, casting a warm glow over the river, Aarohi closed her eyes and made a silent vow. She would carry the essence of this journey within her, using it to guide her actions and decisions. With a heart full of hope and a spirit ready to soar, Aarohi knew she was ready to embrace her purpose and make a difference in the world. She was grateful for Sudha's lessons that taught her that the wonders she had been seeking around were within her, and she was now ready to awaken, nurture, and explore the full potential of 'THE SEVEN WONDERS WITHIN'.

BLURB

YOU CAN'T STOP THE BIRDS OF SADNESS FROM HOVERING OVER YOUR HEAD, BUT YOU CAN DEFINITELY PREVENT THEM FROM NESTING INSIDE YOUR HEAD.

CHANGE YOUR INNER WORLD, AND YOUR OUTER WORLD WILL CHANGE AUTOMATICALLY.

Arriving from the fast-paced world of Canada, Aarohi lands in the spiritual city of Rishikesh, India. Aarohi, a 23-year-old girl, is filled with countless questions about her life as she embarks on a journey to discover its deeper meaning.

One early, pleasant morning on the bank of holy river Ganga, Aarohi meets Sudha and her journey to the inner world begins. Sudha, a spiritual guide to many, thoroughly satisfies Aarohi's curiosity, by answering all her questions with deep insights.

This book is about discovering the true meaning of our lives, identifying what real and lasting happiness in life is and understanding how we can achieve it by transforming our thoughts. It teaches us how to gain control over our thoughts by focusing on our inner selves and outlines a simple, step-by-step approach to growth in all spheres of life.

By applying the methods described in this book, we can strengthen our mental resilience. Through meditation practices focused on various chakras, not only can we find solutions to the biggest challenges in our lives, but we can also achieve our goals and follow a clear path towards eternal peace. Additionally, we can overcome our indecisiveness, short-temperedness and feelings of depression or anxiety.

This book, I would say, leads us to spirituality and shows how we can achieve more in life. By becoming spiritually active, we can make our lives better. This book prepares our inner consciousness so effectively that no question about our lives remains unanswered.

So, get ready for the rejuvenating journey of self-discovery.

– Mr Jignesh Jhaveri

Entrepreneur

For any queries or feedback, contact:

spiritualsoulmates.in
spiritualsoulmatess@gmail.com